OSPREY COMBAT AIRCRAFT • 62

US NAVY PBY CATALINA UNITS OF THE PACIFIC WAR

SERIES EDITOR: TONY HOLMES

OSPREY COMBAT AIRCRAFT • 62

US NAVY PBY CATALINA UNITS OF THE PACIFIC WAR

LOUIS B DORNY

OSPREY PUBLISHING

Front cover
The PBY Catalina achieved many firsts during World War 2, but one of the most dramatic, and least known, is the shooting down of the first Imperial Japanese Navy (IJN) Mitsubishi A6M Zero-sen carrier fighter by a US naval aircraft.

On 10 December 1941, Formosa-based IJN G4M 'Betty' bombers arrived overhead the Cavite Navy Yard in the Philippines just as four PatWing 10 PBY-4 Catalinas were taking off to make a torpedo attack on nearby enemy warships. The bombers' Zero-sen escort engaged two of the PBYs, and as would be observed time and again by Catalina crews during the early stages of the Pacific War, the Japanese pilots proudly showed off their flying abilities with a series of slick aerobatic stunts in the vicinity of the Allied flying-boats.

Lt Harmon Utter and his crew, flying PBY-4 'Boat 2' (BuNo 1238), were set upon by three Tainan *Kokutai* (Air Flotilla) Zero-sens, and one got a little over confident and too close to the flying-boat. The PBY's gunner in the bow, Chief Aviation Machinist Mate and Naval Aviation Pilot (NAP) Earl D Payne, stood up, head and shoulders in the slipstream, and aimed the machine gun forward through the turret mounting. He duly 'filled the engine and pilot's compartment with a long burst from my 0.30-cal Browning'. The maximum effective range of the latter weapon was between 800 and 1000 yards at the most, so the Zero-sen must have been close for Payne to hit it.

The second pilot of PBY 'Boat 28', Ens Ed Bergstrom, had a grandstand seat for the whole event, watching 'the Japanese fighter taking hits, and then suddenly dropping off on one wing and plummeting straight down into Manila Bay'.

That day, all the escorting Tainan *Kokutai* fighters returned to base on Formosa save one – the aircraft flown by Flight Petty Officer Second Class Kojima Tomatsu, who was one of three pilots assigned to attack the PBYs over Manila Bay (*Cover artwork by Mark Postlethwaite*)

First published in Great Britain in 2007 by Osprey Publishing
Midland House, West Way, Botley, Oxford, OX2 0PH
443 Park Avenue South, New York, NY, 10016, USA
E-mail; info@ospreypublishing.com

ISBN 13: 978 1 841769110

Edited by Tony Holmes
Page design by Tony Truscott
Cover Artwork by Mark Postlethwaite
Aircraft Profiles by Jim Laurier
Index by Alan Thatcher
Printed in Hong Kong

07 08 09 10 11 10 9 8 7 6 5 4 3 2 1

For a catalogue of all books published by Osprey please contact:
NORTH AMERICA
Osprey Direct, C/o Random House Distribution Center,
400 Hahn Road, Westminster, MD 21157
E-mail:info@ospreydirect.com

ALL OTHER REGIONS
Osprey Direct UK, PO Box 140 Wellingborough, Northants, NN8 2FA, UK
E-mail: info@ospreydirect.co.uk
www.ospreypublishing.com

CONTENTS

PREPARING FOR WAR

The developmental history of Consolidated's Model 28, better known as the PBY Catalina, is well documented in print, but it is pertinent here to mention that the US Navy's big driver for its creation was the tremendous scouting problem imposed by the vast reaches of the Pacific Ocean. Senior admirals had seen unmistakable signs in their region through the first decades of the twentieth century that a naval war with increasingly militant Japan was on the cards.

In those days, when radar and satellite reconnaissance had not yet even been dreamt of, long-ranging patrol flying-boats were the only means available to solve the US Pacific Fleet's scouting problems. Drawing on its previous experience with the successful P2Y sesquiplane flying-boat of the early 1930s, Consolidated Aircraft created the PBY-1 to see off a rival design from Douglas and win a lucrative US Navy contract in June 1935 for 60 aircraft. Patrol Squadron 11F (VP-11F) duly took delivery of the first examples to reach the frontline in October 1936.

The US Navy quickly realised that it had made the correct choice with the PBY-1, and rapidly began re-equipping its other patrol squadrons. Economic and operational benefits were to be derived by procuring the Consolidated flying-boat in significant numbers, as the unit cost went down and the fleet's ability to conduct long-range patrol missions over greater distances increased. For its day, the PBY-1's performance was impressive – a maximum speed of 179 mph, enclosed cockpits and a range of up to 2000 miles. The US Navy liked what it was getting, and the 60 PBY-1s were soon followed by 50 PBY-2s, 66 PBY-3s and 33 PBY-4s, with each variant offering a slight improvement over the previous model.

The aircraft soon began setting records, with VP-6 establishing the first on 28 January 1937 when all 12 of its PBY-1s made a 2553-mile formation flight directly from San Diego to Ford Island, in Pearl Harbor. This was the beginning of many firsts for the PBY in the Pacific.

Some of the earliest PBY-1s built by Consolidated were delivered to VP-11 in late 1936. Here, '11-P-9' shows its stuff during a sortie from FAB North Island in 1938. The aircraft has standard anti-fouling boot topping on its hull below the waterline and on its floats, as well as insignia blue cowl lower halves (*US Navy*)

The aircraft also proved itself in large-scale exercises held off the west coast of America. During Fleet Problem XIX in 1938, for example, the 'White' (defending) force fielded seven patrol squadrons equipped with PBYs – Patrol Wing (PatWing) 1 had VP-7, VP-9, VP-11 and VP-12, and PatWing 4 controlled VP-16, VP-17 and VP-19. Together, they managed to detect the opposing invading fleet while

VP-8's first six PBY-1s fly in parade formation off San Diego soon after being delivered to the unit in 1937. The black stripes on the hull decking aft and atop the wing were non-skid walkways, while the wing chevron and cowl rings were in red, denoting that these PBYs were assigned to Red Section (*US Navy*)

the latter was still a good distance away from the PBY's base at San Diego, in California. Such detection allowed defending forces to position themselves to advantage. The point was made – the PBY had done the job it had been bought for.

In addition, this exercise saw the US Navy use radio direction finding (RDF, or simply radar, as it was later known) techniques to augment reconnaissance for the first time. RDF involved taking contact bearings from shore stations, ships at sea and from PBYs aloft in an effort to calculate where the enemy was. Even in its rudimentary form, RDF showed considerable promise.

Besides aeroplanes, suitable seaplane tenders and shore base facilities were also essential to support PBY operations, but Depression-era budgets were lean, and few were available. Reasonably well equipped Fleet Air Bases (FABs) existed at North Island (San Diego), Sand Point (Seattle) and Ford Island (Pearl Harbor), with FAB Sitka, in Alaska, under construction in the late 1930s. Naval Air Station (NAS) Alameda, on San Francisco Bay, opened in 1940, and NAS Kaneohe (Oahu) was barely operational by mid-1941, its establishment being spurred by the Pacific Fleet at nearby Pearl Harbor. Lesser Naval Air Facilities (NAF) were in various stages of construction on the west coast, such as Tongue Point, in Oregon, and in the Pacific at Midway, Wake, Johnson, Palmyra, Kodiak, Samoa and Cavite.

USS *Langley* and USS *Wright*, converted from other duties, were the US Navy's only large seaplane tenders until the first built-for-the-purpose vessels USS *Curtiss* and USS *Tangier* joined the Pacific Fleet in mid-1941. In the years prior to the war, several smaller ships were also converted, with a group of *Bird* class minesweepers becoming small tenders. A handful of four-piper destroyers were also converted in 1939-41, whilst the more effective *Barnegat* class tenders joined the fleet in early 1942.

The obvious approach of war, and the equally obvious success of the new PBY-1 in early frontline operations, did much to shape the US Navy's thinking and plans. With an over-the-horizon reach, the PBY was changing the way the fleet did things. Adjustment in organisation led to the directive, on 1 July 1937, that five new patrol wings would be created to control all 18 of the US Navy's VP squadrons. And by the autumn of 1938, all bar four of these

USS *Langley*, seen here at anchor in 1937 off Mare Island, north of San Francisco, was converted from a conventional aircraft carrier into a seaplane tender. The vessel lost part of its forward flightdeck during the conversion. The old girl, known as 'The Covered Wagon' in the Pacific Fleet, was caught and sunk by IJN bombers south of Java on 27 February 1942 (*US Navy*)

units were flying PBYs – VP-14 and VP-15 in Norfolk, Virginia, and VP-18 in Seattle were still equipped with P2Ys, while VP-1 at Pearl Harbor still flew ancient Keystone PK-1 biplane flying-boats.

The patrol wing organisational scheme of 1937 was based on the US Navy's experience with destroyer and submarine flotillas. Once implemented, it proved to be so useful, and flexible, that today's P-3C Orion-equipped patrol wings remain grouped in a similar way.

With the organisational structure firmly in place, the US Navy now looked to force expansion as the way ahead. Although a paucity of funding initially restricted growth, gradually things gained momentum as the political situation both in Europe and the Pacific deteriorated. PatWing 2's VP-1 and VP-18 in Hawaii were among the direct beneficiaries of the Pacific Fleet's plans for expansion when, in late 1938, both units commenced collecting new PBY-4s off Consolidated's San Diego assembly line. The company had delivered some 170+ PBYs by year-end, allowing the Navy to establish two more VP squadrons. Although not all had a full complement of aircraft, let alone PBYs, and more units were planned, Consolidated fulfilled its contractual obligations in May 1939 when it delivered the last of the PBY-4s then on order.

That spring, company engineers commenced work on an alternative to the never quite satisfactory sliding waste hatches in the PBY. They came up with experimental, hand-fashioned, bubble-shaped 'blisters' as replacements, and these were duly fitted to the final three PBY-4s destined for service with VP-18's fourth section – namely '18-P-10' (BuNo 1243), '18-P-11' (BuNo 1242) and '18-P-12' (BuNo 1241).

Ex-World War 1 destroyer USS *Williamson* (photographed here in 1941) gave up its torpedo tubes, three 4-in gun mounts, forward boilers and two stacks when it was converted into a seaplane tender, receiving four twin 20 mm anti-aircraft gun mounts on an enlarged galley deckhouse instead. Vessels such as this provided a workable stand-in until *Barnegat* class tenders joined the fleet (*US Navy*)

PBY-2 BuNo 0466 '2-P-1' was VP-2's lead aircraft, being assigned to the squadron CO. It was photographed on the water off San Diego in 1938 prior to VP-2 being sent to NAS Coco Solo, in the Canal Zone. This aircraft was finally written off when it water-looped during a hard landing in Escambia Bay, Florida, on 15 January 1944 while serving with a training unit (*Naval Institute*)

'Floats up!' '2-P-6' is up on the step and about to take off, and the pilot has given the plane captain the order to retract the wingtip floats. This photograph was taken in the Canal Zone in the late 1930s. VP-2 was a PatWing 3 unit (*US Navy*)

The waist Browning M2 0.50-cal machine guns in early model PBYs were mounted on retractable brackets on either side of the rear fuselage. The starboard weapon is seen here extended, with the sliding waist hatch fully open (*US Navy*)

PBY-4 BuNo 1241 was originally delivered to VP-18 as '18-P-12', before becoming the third aeroplane in VP-13's fourth (Black) section on 1 July 1939 when PatWing 1 took control of the unit. The aircraft remained in San Diego accessible to Consolidated engineers, and was dropped from VP-13 when the squadron returned to Pearl Harbor in December of that year. The PBY-5 contract signed between the US Navy and Consolidated was based on modifications carried out to this PBY-4. Note that although the aircraft features a revised fin/rudder, the elevators still shows VP-13 double green stripes tail marking (*US Navy*)

In addition to the now iconic blisters, '18-P-12' (BuNo 1241) was also fitted with a redesigned rudder that boasted a straight trailing edge, thus greatly improving the PBY's directional stability when in flight.

UNIT RENUMBERING

On 1 July 1939, all units were renumbered to coincide with their wing assignment. For example, VP-17 in PatWing 4 was redesignated VP-42, while PatWing 2's VP-1 and VP-18, now fully re-equipped with PBY-4s, became VP-21 and VP-26, respectively, and returned to Hawaii.

Just weeks after PatWing 2 welcomed its first PBYs in Hawaii, German forces invaded Poland, and President Franklin D Roosevelt ordered the US Navy to commence its now famous Neutrality Patrols. For PatWing 5's PBYs in the Atlantic the heat was now on, whilst in the Pacific, flying-boat

Formerly serving with VP-17, PBY-2 BuNo 0496 became a VP-42 aircraft after the unit's redesignation on 1 July 1939. This unusual view reveals PatWing 4's tail markings, applied to the upper and lower surfaces of the elevator, as well as the rudder. '42-P-7' was the third (Blue) section leader's aircraft, with its incomplete insignia blue wing chevron outlined in white – evidently the wing fabric had been recently changed. The aircraft is also lacking full cowl rings and the section leader's hull band, all of which would be in blue too. The colour of the tail markings remains uncertain (*US Navy*)

A close-up of the port waist blister and Browning M2 0.50-cal machine gun mounting in the PBY-5. The armour plate shield fitted to the weapon became available in early 1942, and was a standard fit fleet-wide by year-end. It gave the exposed gunner some protection from attacking fighters, although the PBY remained incredibly vulnerable to a determined aerial attack throughout World War 2

units were also instructed to increase their patrol distances, with VP-21 being singled out to protect the US Territory of the Philippines from foreign incursions. Having only been back at its Ford Island base for a matter of months, the unit was now tasked with conducting Neutrality Patrol missions from Manila Bay, in the Philippines, in support of the Asiatic Fleet.

VP-21's PBY-4s sit between sorties on the newly completed Sangley Point ramp in January 1940. Note that the anti-fouling paint has been removed from the hull and floats below the waterline on these Philippines-based aircraft (*Ziegler*)

It is worthy of note that the first ever attempt at a transpacific flight by a formation of aircraft of any type was made by VP-21 when it headed to the Philippines at short notice via Midway, Wake and Guam in September 1939 – VP-26 followed in 1940. The PBY-4s managed the flights with little problem, demonstrating yet again in this unprecedented way the mobility of the big flying-boats.

With the introduction of the Neutrality Patrol, there were suddenly shortages everywhere within the US armed forces, and for expanding patrol aviation there were not enough aircraft or aircrew. Requirements quickly outstripped resources, so the US Navy ordered 200 PBY-5s in late 1939 in an effort to remedy its flying-boat shortfall. The PBY-5 was based on the PBY-4, but with fuselage blisters and a modified tail as standard.

While waiting for new orders, Consolidated had continued to perform experimental development work on the very last PBY-4, BuNo 1245, including the fitment of retractable tricycle landing gear that turned the aircraft into an amphibian. Suitably impressed, the US Navy redesignated the aeroplane the XPBY-5A and modified its order so that 33 of the 200 flying-boats under construction would be built as PBY-5As.

Germany's *Blitzkrieg*, President Roosevelt's Neutrality Patrol and the US Navy's order pumped new life into the PBY. The first PBY-5 left the factory in September, after which production quickly increased. Aside from aircraft delivered to the US Navy, export PBYs, dubbed Catalinas, were being built to order for the British, Dutch and Australian air forces.

Although Consolidated had really hit its production straps by late 1940, early PBYs had been forced to shoulder the Neutrality Patrol burden for much of that year. From January 1941 onwards, however,

VP-21's PBY-4 BuNo 1227 '21-P-15' was also photographed on the new seaplane ramp at Sangley Point, again in January 1940. Note the unit's unique Pacific Neutrality Patrol markings that consisted of the national ensign under the outer wing panels and on the hull deck aft of the hatches. National roundels were added to the bow forward of the cockpit in the spring of 1940. This aircraft survived the carnage of the Philippines and the Dutch East Indies, only to be sunk on the water by Zero-sens during a strafing attack on Broome, in Western Australia, on 3 March 1942 (*Ziegler*)

enough PBY-5s, and then PBY-5As, left the assembly line each month to equip at least one and usually as many as three squadrons. Soon, the older PBY-1/2s, now with three or four years of steady usage under their belts, and considered 'over the hill', were passed on to stateside training units.

By December 1941, with new contracts issued by the US Navy, Consolidated had delivered 355 PBY-5/5As to its customers. Just under 300 of these had been supplied to the US Navy, allowing all bar five of its 26 VP squadrons to be issued with PBY-5/5As. Not all were fully equipped, however, with several still transitioning from earlier models. Nevertheless, the PBY-5 was clearly the US Navy's lead flying-boat.

COLOURS

Unit markings in the 1930s made US Navy aircraft some of the most colourful in military service anywhere in the world. Early thinking about the PatWing organisational concept was that they would be regional in nature, and that all squadrons in a given wing would wear similar-pattern tail markings in one of the standard six section colours – insignia red, white, insignia blue, black, lemon yellow and willow green.

PatWing 1 was west coast-based at FAB North Island, and it used different-coloured double horizontal stripes to denote each of its units. PatWing 2 at FAB Pearl, on Ford Island, used solid colours to denote its units, while in the Canal Zone, PatWing 3's PBYs at NAS Coco Solo were marked with a single vertical stripe. PatWing 4, at NAS Sand Point, Seattle, and FAB Sitka, in Alaska, used a chequerboard pattern.

In addition to the five PatWings (PatWing 5 was assigned to the Atlantic Fleet) established in 1937, by early 1941 PatWings 6, 7, 8 and 9 were serving in the Atlantic and PatWing 10 was in the Philippines.

Other than the tail markings previously described, VP units followed the standard paint scheme used by other naval aircraft – bare aluminium overall, chrome yellow upper wings, individual aircraft identifier forward on the bow ('2-P-5', for example, would denote aeroplane No 5 in the wing's second squadron) and wing chevrons, cowl rings and hull bands in section colours. A typical VP unit had 12 PBYs split between four three-aeroplane sections, along with two or three spares. Operational moves and reassignments made for many irregularities in markings, however.

During the winter of 1940-41, with war clearly on the horizon, the US Navy scrapped the high visibility paint schemes of the 1930s, and for the patrol flying-boats the new working uniform was 'non-specular' (flat, no gloss) blue-grey uppersurfaces and flat gull grey on the undersurfaces. 'U.S. Navy' titling was applied on the hull well aft, with the type designator and Bureau Number painted on the fin and the unit aircraft identifier

PBY-2 BuNo 0488 '10-P-11' transferred to PatWing 2's VP-10 from a PatWing 4 squadron in 1938, hence its 'checker tail' markings. VP-10 was always a PatWing 2 squadron, and received PBY-2s in January 1938. It became VP-25 in July 1939, then VP-23 in August 1941, before going to San Diego in November to re-equip with new PBY-5s. BuNo 0488 survived until 25 September 1942, when it water-looped on landing while being flown by a student pilot at NAS Pensacola, Florida, and sank (*US Navy*)

PBY-4 BuNo 1229 '21-P-12' of VP-21 patrols Philippine skies sometime after the June 1940 exchange of aircraft between this unit and VP-26. The aircraft sports the new pattern vertical rudder stripes used in the Asiatic Fleet well into 1941. Note also the PBY's hull stripe and the blue field of the ensign on the hull decking aft. This aircraft was shot down in flames by Zero-sens over Luzon on 10 December 1941 (*Ziegler*)

remaining on the hull below the cockpit. Everything else – section stripes, chevrons and wing tail markings – all went by the board.

In the distant Asiatic Fleet, the Commander-in-Chief devised a camouflage paint scheme for PatWing 10's PBY-4s that remains unique in US naval aviation. Documented only by a few poor-quality photographs, the scheme chosen consisted of several shades of blue, grey and green, according to one PBY veteran, with the exact paints chosen very likely being dictated by the supplies then available in the Philippines.

Early-build PBY-5s were initially delivered in the early silver pre-war scheme, but from late January 1941 onwards all new PBY-5/5As were painted in the blue-grey and gull grey scheme applied in the factory.

Self-sealing fuel tank liners became standard equipment too after the delivery of the first 24 PBY-5s, and although these slightly reduced the flying-boat's fuel capacity, and its maximum range, they were welcomed by crews. The tanks markedly improved the PBY's chances of surviving combat damage by reducing the risk of punctured tanks bursting into flames. Armour plate fittings to the pilots' seat backs and waist gun mountings also offered the crew further protection, and all of these modifications were commonplace in frontline units by mid-1942.

Colour scheme, mission, equipment and base changes were thus daily fare for the patrol squadrons in 1941, and included in the latter was PatWing 1's forward deployment to Kaneohe, in Hawaii, during the summer and autumn months. It left VP-13 behind in San Diego, equipped with the first of Consolidated's new four-engined PB2Y Coronados, as well as some PBYs for the utility and transport roles.

Another change introduced on the eve of war in the Pacific was the US Navy's official adoption of Consolidated's 'Catalina' monicker for the PBY on 1 October 1941.

By the time the Pacific Fleet was attacked in Pearl Harbor on 7 December 1941, the US Navy had 14 VP squadrons in the Pacific, with all bar four of them equipped with PBY-5s. These units, flying a total of 125 PBYs, were split up into four patrol wings that had 17 seaplane tenders to help support seaborne operations. It was a substantial force, yet, in light of the coming challenge of war, well short of what was required. Through the summer months of 1941 some units were split to facilitate growth, while others were established from scratch.

VP-102's PBY-4 BuNo 1226 on the ramp at Olongapo, in the Philippines, provides the backdrop for ACMM Francis Crombie and his fellow crewmembers who subsequently dropped these wreaths in the South China Sea on Memorial Day 1941. 'Boat 22' has been painted in Asiatic Fleet camouflage and adorned with dark grey numerals. This PBY was forced down with worn out engines and abandoned in the Dutch East Indies in January 1942 (*Bud Williford*)

PBY-4 BuNo 1233 'Boat 8' of VP-101 was also resprayed in the Asiatic Fleet's unique local camouflage pattern. PatWing 10 in the Philippines had repainted all 28 of its PBY-4s (flown by VP-101 and VP-102) in variations of this scheme by the time war came to the Pacific in December 1941. 'Boat 8' was sunk on the water at Darwin on 19 February 1942 (*Ziegler*)

VP-52's '52-P-1' gets a wash down, probably at NAS Norfolk in mid-1941. Several of the unit's PBY-5s were transferred to VP-51 in late 1941 and then flown to Pearl Harbor when the squadron was hastily sent west in the immediate aftermath of the 7 December attack. Once in Hawaii, VP-51 passed on its aircraft to VP-22, which in turn headed for Australia

SECRET SURVEY FLIGHTS

With the political situation in the Pacific rapidly deteriorating, the US Navy clearly recognised that PatWing 10 in the Philippines was at the far end of a tenuous supply line, and in the event of war it could not long sustain itself. In addition, the US Army Air Forces (USAAF) wanted to establish a South Pacific ferry route to move more heavy bombers to the Philippines. In response, Commander Task Force (CTF) 9 had VP-22 carry out a survey flight in August across the South Pacific as far as Darwin, in northern Australia, to seek out alternative supply routes.

The operation was carried out as clandestinely as possible, as no one wanted to alert the Japanese. Thanks to a close working relationship with the Australian armed forces, the survey flights proved to be very successful. Two PBY-3s were involved, with Lt Cdr Frank O'Beirne commanding '22-P-1' and Lt Tom Moorer flying '22-P-10'. Each carried a clutch of USAAF officers who were briefed to find locations suitable for supporting B-17 Flying Fortress operations. These men quickly established that the pioneering South Pacific route was not only feasible, but that existing facilities, though still sparse and inadequate, showed sufficient promise to allow the route to be developed so that it could handle ferry traffic.

The PBY-3s completed this mission without any drama, and the US Navy also benefited from its involvement in the operation as it too was interested in the South Pacific. Indeed, naval officers, in conjunction with the Australians, surveyed potential remote anchorages in the Santa Cruz Islands – work that later proved very useful.

In the weeks immediately prior to the Pearl Harbor attack, Oahu-based Catalinas, primarily from VP-21 and VP-22, scouted two million square miles of Pacific Ocean. Daily, patrols were flown by the latter unit, with operations from Midway Island often stretching as far as 700 miles from base. On 1 December CTF 9 directed VP-21 to start relieving VP-22 of this onerous task by

VP-22's PBY-3 BuNo 0858 '22-P-10' was photographed at Darwin, in Australia's Northern Territory, in August 1941 in the middle of the clandestine South Pacific survey flight jointly carried out by the US Navy and the USAAF. Lt Tom Moorer was the PBY's pilot and AMM3c Chuck Baggarly its plane captain. '22-P-10' was destroyed on the ramp at NAS Ford Island on the morning of 7 December 1941 (*LeBaron Baggarly*)

sending its PBYs first to Johnson Island to refuel and then north to Midway in 'scouting line' formation – e.g. two or more PBYs flying parallel, spaced up to 30 miles apart, depending on visibility. When flown in such a formation, VP-21 could scan a swath of ocean 200 miles wide.

According to senior naval officers in the Pacific Fleet, the most significant threat they faced was an enemy fleet attack launched from the Japanese-controlled Marshall Islands, south of Wake Island, and it was against this threat that VP-21's flight was guarding.

VP-22, when relieved on Midway, was ordered to fly a similar scouting line search on 3 December from Wake Island. One of the unit's PBYs duly flew out some 200 miles to meet the aircraft carrier USS *Enterprise* to provide a navigational escort for 12 F4F Wildcats from VMF-211 that were flying in from the vessel to augment the island's garrison. Once this mission was accomplished, VP-22 flew another scouting line from Wake Island back to Pearl Harbor, arriving in Hawaii late in the afternoon of 5 December. Nothing had been sighted by either squadron.

In the Philippines, meanwhile, PatWing 10's PBY-4s were flying long patrols west to Vichy French Indochina, east to the Marshall Islands and north to Formosa so as to monitor Japanese fleet movements whenever possible. One scouting flight was laid on to reconnoitre the remote Spratley Islands, in the South China Sea, and the PBY flew out with instructions to break off and report by radio if enemy fighters were encountered. They found nothing there, either. The situation proved to be different on Formosa, however, where IJN fighter pilots were foiled in their attempts to intercept US Navy Catalinas flying photo missions over their bases on the island by poor weather.

Through early December, PBYs patrolling off the Indochina coast spotted many merchant ships that looked suspiciously like an invasion force gathering in Cam Rahn Bay. The patrol on 5 December found the harbour empty! This information was immediately flashed to Washington, D.C., and it was also passed on to the British command in Singapore. Royal Air Force patrols soon spotted the Japanese vessels heading south-west, and the Royal Navy's Force Z sailed to intercept them.

Late November and early December 1941 was an extraordinary time for Pacific PBY units, with tensions running high on the eve of war.

This rare in-flight view of a camouflaged PatWing 10 PBY-4 was taken from another Catalina over the Dutch East Indies in 1941-42 (*Ziegler*)

PEARL HARBOR

The pressures of maintaining the Neutrality Patrol, and searching for marauding U-boats in the Atlantic despite the USA not technically being a belligerent, had tended to draw precious PBY resources eastward from September 1939. The Japanese attack on Hawaii on the morning of Sunday, 7 December 1941 changed that in a heartbeat.

CTF 9 Pacific Fleet/Commander PatWing 2, Rear Admiral P N L Bellinger, had 81 PBYs under his command by December 1941. Some 54 of these were brand new PBY-5s just ferried in over the previous weeks, and still inadequately supported for sustained operations. Four of VP-23's PBY-5s had been deployed south to patrol from Palmyra and Johnson islands, while VP-21 was temporarily flying from Midway.

Although 81 PBYs represented a sizeable force, PatWing 2's chances of spotting an approaching fast carrier attack force in the vast western Pacific were slim at best. The latter would most likely approach Hawaii from the northern, western or southern quadrants during the hours of darkness at speeds approaching 30 knots. The vessels would aim to be in position some 150-200 miles from Pearl Harbor so as to be able to launch their aircraft at dawn.

In order to adequately patrol the western half of the compass (180 through to 000 degrees) in five sectors out to a distance of 200 miles at dawn, some 36 PBYs would have had to have launched from Hawaii in the middle of the night on eight- to ten-hour patrols for weeks at a time. And this operational tempo could only have been sustained if the entire eastern half of the Hawaiian islands were left unscouted. The professional airmen of PatWing 2 believed such intense operations were indeed doable, but only if the PBY units they staffed boasted fully trained personnel and adequate maintenance and support facilities. Sadly, CTF 9 fell short in all three departments!

At any rate, sabotage was then considered to pose a greater threat to the Pacific Fleet than aerial attack, with a thrust north by Japanese battleships and cruisers based in the Marshall Islands of equal concern. Theoretically, an air strike was possible, but most senior officers considered it very unlikely. Reflecting the fleet commander's anxieties, VP-21 on Midway had seven aeroplanes patrolling sectors to the southeast (120 through 170 degrees) of the island out to a distance of 450 miles on the morning of 7 December. Four more PBY-3s were anchored in the lagoon, each one armed with two 500-lb bombs, on ten minutes' notice to take-off. The twelfth flying-boat was being serviced ashore in the squadron hangar.

Back in Hawaii, the training of new personnel to help with the rapid expansion of PatWing 2 had placed an additional burden on the established PBY units that now found themselves frantically patrolling the Pacific in search of a potential foe. Routine daylight sector searches were now typically being extended out to 500 miles in selected areas, although potentially dangerous night operations were still far from routine in late 1941.

And under the cover of darkness, the IJN's *Kido Butai* – the six-carrier Pearl Harbor attack force under the command of Admiral Chuichi Nagumo – raced through the night to the planned dawn launch position some 240 miles north-northwest of Oahu without being detected.

At Pearl Harbor and Kaneohe on the morning of 7 December 1941, the PBY squadrons were in varying degrees of readiness. VP-11 had 12 aeroplanes ready for flight on four hours' notice and VP-12 had six PBYs ready for flight on 30 minutes' notice, with five more on four hours' notice. VP-14 had three Catalinas in the air on security patrols, each of them armed with depth charges. Three others were back at base on 30 minutes' notice, with four more on four hours' notice. All of VP-22's aircraft were on four hours' notice, as were 11 of VP-23's PBYs. Finally, VP-24 had four flying-boats in the air conducting inter-type exercises with submarines east of Oahu, and a fifth PBY was ready for flight on 30 minutes' notice.

Elsewhere, the seaplane tender USS *Wright* was en route to Hawaii from Midway after off-loading cargo, with all the remaining tenders in port at Pearl Harbor.

FIRST SHOTS IN ANGER

Shortly after 0600 hrs on 7 December, VP-14's PBY '14-P-1' had departed NAS Kaneohe as part of the unit's duty patrol for that day. Ens William Tanner was in command of the aircraft, and he was both a little anxious to be flying his CO's Catalina and very conscious of the warning he had been given in the pre-mission briefing – 'be very alert during this period of great tension'. He also knew that although the alert status had been relaxed elsewhere, it remained at the highest peacetime level in the defensive area off the entrance to Pearl Harbor. Tanner's PBY carried live depth charges under each wing to further emphasise this point.

Once '14-P-1' was in the defensive area, it spotted the supply vessel USS *Antares* steering for the harbour entrance channel with its gunnery target tow immediately behind it. Just minutes later the PBY crew spotted a strange object in the water between the supply ship and its tow, very clearly outside the submarine sanctuary areas. The PBY nosed over to get a better view, dropped smoke floats near the intruder and, by doing so, attracted, or at least heightened, the attention of the duty destroyer USS *Ward*. An alert lookout on the vessel also noticed the strange object as well, and the PBY saw the destroyer turn towards the intruder almost immediately, bearing down fast.

Tanner then also attacked the submerged object, bracketing it with two depth charges – his radioman immediately reported this attack to Pearl Harbor. At much the same time *Ward* went to general quarters and attacked the target with gunfire, then steered to ram. It also dropped depth charges on the intruder, advising the Commandant of the 14th Naval District of this development at 0630 hrs.

From the PBY's vantage point, nothing more was seen of what turned out to be a Japanese midget submarine, which was almost certainly sunk by this combined attack. Aloft, Ens Tanner could not be sure of the vessel's demise, however, leaving him filled with mixed emotions. Yes, the submarine was clearly in the wrong place, but what if it was a US Navy vessel? Had he just killed American sailors? He and the remaining two

PBYs that were operating under his direction continued their patrols to the south of Oahu.

Just over an hour later, a few minutes before 0800 hrs, the voice radio circuits in the PBYs came alive with excited, confused traffic. Pearl Harbor was under air attack!

Subsequently, '14-P-1' received a coded message, which Tanner's radioman properly challenged for authentication. His three PBYs were assigned to search 30 sectors from 270 to 360 degrees (to the northwest of Oahu) to the extent of their fuel and report back what they found – this instruction revealed that the command at Kaneohe was recovering from the shock of the raid and now taking action in response. Tanner made the assignments on the spot, giving Ens Fred Meyers in '14-P-2' the 330-360 degrees sector.

He and his crew were about 40 miles north of Oahu when they sighted dozens of aircraft dead ahead. The Japanese A6M Zero-sen fighters turned back to attack the PBY, but being low on both ammunition and fuel, they soon left the flying-boat alone and continued on their way to their respective carriers. With hindsight, Meyers' radio report was almost certainly the most accurate indicator of the direction from which the attackers had come, but this detail was lost in the flurry of activity back in Hawaii.

Bill Tanner's '14-P-1' had been the first US aircraft to fire on the enemy and Fred Meyers' '14-P-2' the first US Navy aircraft aloft to be fired on during the Pacific War.

PEARL HARBOR ATTACK

The first bombs fell on the Ford Island seaplane ramp very near VP-22's parked PBY-3s, and in no time at all almost all of the aeroplanes on the island had been destroyed. Cdr Logan Ramsey, PatWing 2's chief of staff, rushed into the radio room in the headquarters building and, amid the explosions of bombs, shouted the implied orders to the radioman on watch – 'Air Raid Pearl Harbor. This is no drill!' This electrifying signal soon passed across oceans and continents.

At nearby Kaneohe, strafing Zero-sen fighters soon reduced the base to a shambles. VP-11 had been ready to depart the next morning on an advanced base exercise to Johnson Island, and its aircraft were parked in lines neatly alongside some VP-12 Catalinas on the ramp. Still more PBYs were anchored out in the bay, simulating being on advanced base operations for training and readiness drills. In minutes they were all in flames. The carnage was staggering, and although damage to maintenance and accommodation facilities was not major, PatWing 2's capacity to mount patrols in retaliation was reduced to zero, just as the Japanese had intended.

Two brand new seaplane tenders were moored on the west side of

A damaged PBY-5 is pulled away from other burning flying-boats at NAS Pearl Harbor on the morning of Sunday, 7 December 1941. The fabric covering the wing of this anonymous Catalina appears to have been entirely burned away (*US Navy*)

Stunned sailors watch explosions on Ford Island. To their right is the charred remains of a PBY wing, whilst in the middle distance is a more intact Catalina, as well as an OS2U Kingfisher and an SOC Seagull

Ford Island, with USS *Tangier* near the battleship USS *Utah* and USS *Curtiss* directly across the channel from these vessels. The explosions on Ford Island quickly alerted the crews of both tenders that Pearl Harbor was under attack, and a number of sailors aboard *Tangier* later stated that their ship was the first to open fire at the Japanese aircraft. Almost certainly the machine that crashed into *Curtiss* during the attack had been badly hit by the machine gunners aboard *Tangier* as it flew by at low altitude.

A PBY-5 burns at NAS Kaneohe soon after the 7 December attack

The four VP-24 PBYs operating from Lahaina Roads, off nearby Maui, learned of the attack by radio, and their first reaction was to return to Ford Island. However, the squadron CO instead chose to fly a series of search

Another NAS Kaneohe PBY-5 is heaved into the shallows by officers and ratings alike before the flying-boat sinks at its moorings, the aircraft having already lost its port wing to a fuel fire started by strafing Zero-sens

The brand new seaplane tender USS *Curtiss* was struck by a crashing enemy aircraft during the attack, although the subsequent blaze seen burning in this photograph was quickly put out by the crew. The vessel was only lightly damaged (although 20 sailors were killed), and it sailed to support PBY patrols in the South Pacific within weeks of the attack (*US Navy*)

This photograph of the NAS Pearl Harbor ramp was taken shortly after the attack had ended. The destroyer USS *Shaw* is still burning in the Navy Yard, and the masts of grounded battleship USS *Nevada* can be seen to the right. Sailors have already begun recovery operations on the flightline around the PBY-5 and the fire-scarred Curtiss SOC on beaching gear (US Navy)

sectors, and one of the unit's crews attacked what was probably a Japanese submarine some miles south of Barber's Point but found no further trace of the enemy. The squadron commander in '24-P-1', along with '24-P-4' and two other aircraft, recovered at Ford Island late in the day, taxiing through the wreckage and oil to the seaplane ramp at their now-devastated base.

On Midway, the news of the attack on Pearl Harbor came like a lightning bolt, but was not received with undue surprise, as the island had essentially been on a war footing in any case. Dutch Navy Catalina Y 70 was being ferried to the East Indies via Midway at the time, and it was promptly commandeered.

The track of the *Kido Butai* was, of course, well away from Midway, since the Japanese had guessed correctly that PBYs would be based on the islands, and they were fully aware of the aircraft's long range. Indeed, the only carrier in the immediate vicinity was the Pacific Fleet's USS *Lexington*, which was approaching Midway with Marine Corps scout-bomber squadron VMSB-231 embarked. Two VP-21 PBYs launched on the morning of 7 December to intercept the vessel and escort the Marine Corps SBD Dauntlesses to the island. However, upon learning of the attack on Pearl Harbor, the skipper of *Lexington* chose to keep the unit embarked for the moment and search for the Japanese force himself. None of these patrols found anything, however.

Despite various aircraft conducting operations around Midway, two Japanese destroyers succeeded in getting in close enough to the island base during the evening of 7 December and shelled the airfield. A hangar was destroyed, as was the solitary PBY-3 that was undergoing minor repairs within it.

VP-21's PBY-3 BuNo 0823 was destroyed when NAS Midway was shelled by IJN vessels on the evening of 7 December 1941. The hangar the flying-boat was housed in was also destroyed

Twenty-four hours after the raid, a PBY from VP-21 flew an afternoon patrol from Johnson Island back to Pearl Harbor. At 1618 hrs its crew reported sighting and bombing an enemy cruiser and destroyer south east of Johnson. The targets were, in fact, the heavy cruiser USS *Portland* and destroyer USS *Porter*, which were in turn part of Rear Admiral Wilson Brown's TF 12. *Lexington* was just a few miles away, and the cruiser had dropped out of formation several hours earlier in order to recover the crew of a ditched aeroplane.

The carrier launched an additional Combat Air Patrol made up of ten VF-2 F2A-3 Buffalos, which were sent to *Portland's* assistance. The cruiser got off some flak rounds, but missed, and luckily for the PBY, it was correctly identified by the US Navy fighter pilots before they shot it out of the sky.

When VP-21 returned to Ford Island from Midway on 13 December, little repair work had been carried out on the base. The next day, the air group from USS *Saratoga*, hurrying from the west coast, flew into Kaneohe. Upon his arrival at the base, a naval aviator remarked;

NAS Kaneohe is seen from the air on 9 December 1941. The damage to the naval air station is clearly evident, as are six seemingly intact PBYs

'Our first glimpse of the damage showed the skeletons of burned and bombed PBYs. They had been piled to one side in the week since the attack. The framework of a burned-out hangar still stood gauntly black in the sunshine. The wreckage of two or three machine-gunned and burned-out cars still stood beside the road. Broken glass had been cleared away, but bullet holes still scarred the plaster of the BOQ.'

PatWings' 1 and 2 had 68 PBYs present on Oahu at the time of the attack, and all bar a dozen at most were either destroyed, damaged or left unflyable.

Having dealt the Pacific Fleet a near-fatal blow at Pearl Harbor, the IJN now turned its attention to tiny Wake Island in the western Pacific. Although no PBYs were permanently based here, an aircraft from VP-22 had briefly visited the island just prior to the 7 December attack. Catalinas sporadically flew in and out of Wake until 21 December, and the last contact the outside world had with the embattled defenders on the island came via a PBY-5 on this date. The garrison finally surrendered two days later.

REBUILDING THE PBY FORCE

The terrible devastation in Hawaii did, nevertheless, allow the patrol aviation community to showcase the utility of their long-range flying-boats. Four Atlantic PBY squadrons were immediately sent to the Pacific, whilst Pacific Fleet at Pearl Harbor was ordered to send a VP squadron west to augment PatWing 10.

VP-51, VP-71 and VP-72 departed for Hawaii within hours of the attack, followed by VP-91 the following day. At Ford Island, VP-22, having just started their transition training onto the PBY-5, took charge of 12 Catalinas flown in by VP-51 and departed on 2 January 1942 for the Philippines via the South Pacific ferry route.

One that did not survive at NAS Kaneohe – VP-12's PBY-5 '12-P-3' was fit only for scrapping

PBY-5s sit on their beaching gear on the apron at NAS Pearl Harbor, looking south, with the grounded battleship *Nevada* in the background (*US Navy*)

Once the unit reached Darwin, where the seaplane tender USS *Langley* was homeported as the aviation station ship for the region, VP-22 would switch operational commands from the Pacific to the Asiatic Fleet. The squadron then flew on to join up with VP-101 and VP-102 in the Philippines.

Back in Hawaii, VP-71 and VP-72 quickly settled into operations from battle-scarred Kaneohe, performing long-range patrol tasks as directed. VP-91 paused briefly at Alameda, in California, en route, but subsequently joined PatWing 1 at Kaneohe in February 1942. The unit would remain in Hawaii conducting regular patrols until September. With the arrival of these units in Hawaii, the western Pacific was now being covered, albeit thinly, by PBYs once again.

Maintenance and repair crews at both Ford Island and Kaneohe struggled to patch together what could be salvaged and repaired from the original fleet of PBYs, all the while supporting the new squadrons that had been flown in. Their ingenuity and hard work eventually paid dividends, as a small number of rebuilt PBY-5s were created from the many damaged flying-boats left in the wake of the raid. Enough aircraft had been returned to service by February 1942 to allow VP-21 to send its older PBY-3s – the last in the Pacific – back to the US and re-equip with 12 'new' PBY-5s.

A surviving PatWing 2 PBY-5 heads out from Hawaii on a patrol in early 1942, the aircraft boasting early war markings, but not the red rudder stripes. The latter were worn by most PBYs between December 1941 and May 1942

PATWING 10's ORDEAL

As bad as the attack had been for the PBY units in Hawaii, their ordeal had lasted little more than two hours. For PatWing 10, its ill-fated campaign in defence of the Philippines commenced on 7 December and lasted until Corregidor finally fell on 6 May 1942.

US military targets in Luzon were initially attacked by Formosa-based Japanese bombers, escorted by A6M Zero-sens. The latter outfought the USAAF's 24th Pursuit Group, securing air superiority, which in turn allowed all airfields to be knocked out of action. On 10 December, enemy bombers started to target other military installations, including the navy yard at Cavite, which was set ablaze during an unopposed noon raid.

PatWing 10's long patrols to detect approaching enemy vessels were, despite some minor contacts, of no avail until the morning of 10 December, when VP-102's 'Boat 17', flying from Subic, sighted two 'battleships'. These turned out to be the heavy cruisers *Ashigara* and *Maya*. Five PBY-4s attacked the vessels with bombs during the first US Navy air strike on surface ships of the Japanese fleet. A further four torpedo-equipped PBYs from VP-101 were in the process of taking off in a follow up attack when Japanese bombers appeared overhead and targeted the navy yard. Escorting Zero-sen fighters immediately honed in on 'Boat 2', flown by Lt Harmon Utter, and 'Boat 28', with Ens Robert McConnell at the controls. Both flying-boats were forced down with battle damage, while Ens Russell Snyder's 'Boat 12' crashed in flames.

Despite the loss of a PBY, VP-101 achieved another first for the Catalina during this one-sided clash when 'Boat 2' managed to down a Japanese fighter. Twisting and turning the big flying-boat so as to put the Zero-sen pilots off their aim, Lt Utter steadied the PBY just long enough for bow gunner Chief Aviation Machinist Mate (NAP) Earl D Payne to fire at an enemy fighter that was literally filling his gun sight. Firing off a long burst of 0.30-cal rounds from his machine gun, Payne's bullets struck the cockpit and engine of the enemy aircraft, which fell away on one wing with its fuselage on fire, The aeroplane subsequently plunged into Manila Bay. Ens Ed Bergstrom, in 'Boat 28', confirmed the fighter's demise, thus giving credit for the first Zero-sen to be brought down by a US Navy aircraft in the Pacific War to VP-101's PBY-4 BuNo 1238.

Despite this success, two days later marauding IJN fighters sank no fewer than seven PBYs anchored in Subic Bay near the naval station at Olongapo. For Asiatic Fleet Commander-in-Chief Admiral Thomas C Hart, this loss convinced him that PatWing 10's surviving Catalinas could not remain in the Philippines. He promptly ordered wing CO Capt Frank D Wagner to fly his remaining aeroplanes south to Ambon, in the Dutch East Indies, to operate alongside Dutch Catalinas.

The wing's 11 surviving PBYs left the Philippines on 15 December, although they continued to support American forces in the region. In the pre-dawn darkness of 27 December, six PBYs from VP-101 set off in two flights of three on an 800-mile roundtrip to attack enemy shipping anchored off Jolo Island. Unfortunately for them, A6Ms of the Tainan *Kokutai* had flown into an airstrip on the island just the day before. Patrolling overhead the vessels, eight fighters quickly engaged the PBYs. Chief Machinist's Mate Mike Kelly, who was part of the crew onboard Lt John Hyland's PBY, which was leading the second section, recalled;

'We started in on our bombing run and the machine-gunner aft in my aeroplane reported fighters above, and plenty of them. They started to dive on us immediately, but we held our course and went in to bomb the vessels below. The other section of our squadron had already made a nice approach and dropped their bombs. We came in with fierce anti-aircraft fire breaking all around us. Yes, and some of it through us. Our gunners were keeping the Japs off as well as they could as we dived for the water.

'One PBY in our section was shot down. A Jap made a run for us from underneath, and our tunnel gun knocked him off as pretty as you could imagine. The Japs must have concluded that was a bad spot – to come at us from underneath – so they changed tactics and attacked us from above.

'Only my aeroplane and one other from my section got back to base. None of the other section returned. Four aeroplanes were lost.'

The missing PBY from Lt Hyland's section was '101-P-11', which had been forced down onto the sea. Amongst is crew was Chief Machinist's Mate John Cumberland, who remembers;

'We made our turn and came in over the Jap fleet. Then we ran for one of their destroyers. We bombed for a near-miss, then made another turn for altitude. Just then the enemy fighters came after us. One of them came in under the stabiliser. I held off until he got in good range, then fanned my string of fire at him. It apparently did no good, for he came right back again, and with him were half-a-dozen others.

'They would make a run for our starboard, then our port side. I hit one of them, a "Zero", fair in the belly. Our own ship was filling up – with holes. By the time we got it down onto the water, most of the crew were gas-drunk from leakage.'

VP-101's '101-P-1', '101-P-6' and '101-P-9', which were all part of Lt Burden Hastings' flight, were shot down off Jolo, with only a handful of survivors, whilst '101-P-11' came down some distance away from the island. The flying-boat remained afloat, and its crew were rescued the following day by another PBY that had picked up distress signals being broadcast by the aircraft.

VP-21's PBY-4 BuNo 1240 '21-P-6' performs a Neutrality Patrol over the Philippines in mid-1940. It has white cowl lower halves, an Asiatic Fleet rudder flash and a faded centre to its insignia. This aircraft was one of four PBYs downed by Zero-sens off Jolo, in the Philippines, on 27 December 1941 (*Ziegler*)

VP-21's PBY-4 BuNo 1218 '21-P-8' sits at anchor off Sangley Point shortly after the squadron's arrival in the Philippines in September 1939. The aircraft is still wearing VP-21's solid red rudder marking. BuNo 1218 was later assigned to VP-102 as 'Boat 28', and it was shot down over Kema, in the Northern Celebes, on 11 January 1942 (*Ziegler*)

A fifth PBY ('102-P-28') from PatWing 10 was downed by an F1M floatplane fighter on 11 January 1942 when four US Navy Catalinas and three Dutch flying-boats were sent to attack the Japanese invasion force landing troops at Kema, in the Northern Celebes.

The painful lesson learned from these missions was that the PBY was virtually helpless against determined fighter attack. The USAAF's heavy bombers, which had also been withdrawn from the Philippines to Java to support the East Indies campaign, were also learning the same lesson. Indeed on 17 January, at first light, three LB-30 Liberators and two B-17E Flying Fortresses from the combined 7th/19th Bomb Group (BG) attacked the Japanese invasion force at Menado, in the Dutch Celebes. There was no interception over the target, but as the bombers turned for home, the A6Ms of the 3rd *Kokutai* fell on the USAAF 'heavies'. Two made it back to Java badly shot up and two others were forced down, but the fifth aeroplane, LB-30 AL535, simply vanished.

More than a week later, a B-17 searching for enemy vessels in the Java Sea overflew the small island of Greater Mesalembo and noticed the wreckage of a large bomber in its lagoon. The crew immediately reported what they had found, and PatWing 10 was asked by the USAAF to send a PBY to the area to pick up any survivors. 'Boat 42' (ex-Dutch Navy Model 28-5MN) happened to be returning from a patrol in the area, so it was diverted to Greater Mesalembo. Once over the island, the wind in the area was not severe, but the sea appeared treacherous, with swells several feet high and breaking as they approached the island. The pilot, Lt D A Campbell, jettisoned his two bombs so as to improve the flying-boat's handling on the water, and then circled to make an upwind approach.

Once on the water, the danger was not past, as the island had no high ground. This made it hard for the pilot on the water to judge his distance from the breaking surf. The wind was up and the waves much higher than they seemed from the air. The PBY's radioman atop the wing signalled ashore, and the bomber crew – eight men, of whom two were wounded – quickly shoved off through the surf in their rubber raft and worked their way out to the flying-boat a half-mile offshore. After what seemed like hours of waiting, the crew back aft eventually got the raft alongside and wrestled the eight men through the blister.

The PBY crewmen knew what was coming, so they quickly got the rescuees secured in positions for take-off as the Catalina surged forward into the wind and began plunging through seemingly solid walls of green Java Sea. Slowly gathering speed, and shaking off one wave only to crash into the crest of the next, the aircraft began to pop rivets and blow out patches over bullet holes in the hull. Despite the relentless pounding, the PBY made it off. By now both the rescued and the rescuers were soaked to the skin, but the water within the

A camouflaged PBY-4 of PatWing 4 patrols over the Dutch East Indies in 1941-42, its crew relying on low-level cloud to help it remain concealed from IJN fighters (*Ziegler*)

aeroplane soon began to drain away thanks to the slipstream, the popped rivets and reopened bullet holes.

The PBY had rescued the missing LB-30 crew from the 11th BS/7th BG, which was beginning to lose hope after nine days of isolation on a remote island. With all their food and water gone, and in need of medicines for the wounded, the crew's prayers had been answered when the PBY alighted just off Greater Mesalembo.

MORE LOSSES

In the Dutch East Indies, one tragedy followed close on another. Having lost five PBYs in operations from the seaplane base at Ambon, PatWing 10's operational strength was reaching crisis point. Fortunately, VP-22 joined the remnants of this force just in the nick of time, having arrived in the East Indies from Hawaii via Darwin. It started flying combat patrols within 24 hours of arriving at Ambon, but like VP-101, VP-22 also lost aircraft to marauding Zero-sens. Indeed, two PBYs ('22-P-7' and '22-P-8') were shot down in flames by six fighters from the 3rd *Kokutai* as they came in to land at the Halong seaplane base on 15 January.

VP-101 exacted some revenge for PatWing 10 the following day when the PBY flown by Ens John F Davis was intercepted by a solitary A6M over the Gulf of Tomini. The flying-boat suffered a number of hits, but emerged victorious, as recalled by Chief Machinist's Mate Van Bibber;

'We were off the coast of the Celebes when a fighter dove on us. We were at about 10,000 ft. We saw him coming in time to start sliding right towards him, and just about the time he bounced us, we put our aeroplane into a slipping dive. He overshot us. Every time he would start back for us, we'd repeat the dive.

'The Jap made four runs, firing as he passed over. The fourth time he must have been in a hurry, for he started to turn back on us too soon. This brought him right above our quarter – wide open for a "Sunday shot". Our waist gunner filled the Jap's cockpit with bullets. The Jap at once fell off on a wingtip and started smoking. It rolled over and plunged down about a thousand feet before it burst into flames.'

This success was in isolation, however, as the unrelenting pressure of the enemy advance and the lack of proper logistics and maintenance for the PBYs cost PatWing 10 heavily. Altogether, seven flying-boats were lost to fighters during patrols and five more on abortive bombing attempts during the ill-fated defence of the Dutch East Indies. A further 19 PBYs were destroyed on the water or ashore by enemy aircraft.

Four of the aircraft lost to fighters were destroyed on 19 February during the devastating carrier strike on Darwin. The first to go down was VP-22's '22-P-18', flown by Lt Thomas Moorer. One of a pair of PBYs sent on patrol by the tender USS *William B Preston*, the aircraft was despatched by an A6M from the carrier *Kaga*. The remaining three PBYs lost were sunk at their moorings off Bathurst Island when strafed.

William B Preston's second PBY ('22-P-10'), flown by Lt(jg) Robert 'Buzz' LeFever, escaped the attentions of the fighters and, unexpectedly, spotted the *Kido Butai* in the holding area 240 miles north-northwest of Darwin in the Timor Sea whilst steering for their patrol sector off Dutch Timor. 'Buzz' and his crew were the first Americans to catch sight of the carriers that had attacked Pearl Harbor some ten weeks earlier.

This photo of Admiral Thomas H Moorer was taken shortly before his retirement as the Chairman of the Joint Chiefs of Staff in 1974 following 41 years of active service. Three decades earlier, he had seen plenty of combat whilst serving as a PBY commander in the Pacific Fleet. Moorer was at Pearl Harbor with VP-22 on 7 December 1941, where his PBY was destroyed on the ramp. Over the next 90 days he had seen the same Japanese aeroplanes twice more in action – at Ambon, in the Dutch East Indies, and off Darwin when Zero-sens from the carrier *Hiryu* shot him down in flames on 19 February 1942 (*US Navy*)

Five crewmen from VP-102's 'Boat 27', PBY-4 BuNo 1214, pose at NAS Sangley Point in the autumn of 1941. In the back row are Ens Charles Van Dusen, ACMM Tommy Dunn and RM2c Miller, whilst in the front row are AMM3c Bud Williford and third pilot AMM1c (NAP) Don Dixon. This aircraft later became 'Boat 4', and it was sunk on the water at Darwin on 19 February 1942 (*Bud Williford*)

The enemy, powerful and constantly advancing under the cover of strong fighter protection, posed a particularly difficult challenge to patrolling PBYs and their crews. Against the skilful, aggressive IJN fighter pilots, the Catalina was terribly vulnerable – too slow, too lightly armed, poorly protected without armour or self-sealing fuel tanks and vulnerable to machine gun and cannon fire. The knocks endured by the PatWings during this campaign, and in the Philippines, contributed to the US Navy's decision to buy higher performance land-based PB4Y bombers (a navalised version of the B-24 Liberator) rather than more flying-boats.

But all this lay in the future. For PatWing 10 in early 1942, its units had little choice but to continue their patrols in search of the enemy. Things got so bad that the crews in Java dubbed the patrol sector into Makassar Straits 'Cold Turkey Lane', but the missions had to continue, for Allied commanders had no other source for the critical information that they required in order to keep track of enemy shipping and troop movements.

On 24 February yet another PBY failed to return from 'Cold Turkey Lane', 'Boat 42', flown by Lt John Robertson, spotting a convoy of ships anchored off Makassar, in the Celebes. At 1410 hrs, near Balikpapan, the radio watch in Java copied the following plain text signal from the PBY;

'Being attacked by aircraft north. Many ships in fleet . . .'

The transmitted signal appeared to have been cut off in mid-sentence, which almost certainly meant that the PBY had been set upon by two A6Ms from the Tainan *Kokutai* that were patrolling overhead the convoy. The radio watch in Java quickly responded, and 'rogered' for the signal, asking for a position from Radioman First Class John Simpson or Radioman Second Class Vernon Failer. Exactly where the PBY was at the time is unclear, but it was certainly in the vicinity of Balikpapan.

The PatWing 10 commander later stated that 'Boat 42's' discovery of the convoy led directly to the upcoming Battle of the Java Sea. The 'Many ships in fleet' call was certainly referring to the 41 Japanese transports, and their escorts, that the PBY had spotted heading south from Jolo and Davao carrying troops for the invasion of eastern Java.

Java radio watch waited for an answer, then asked again, and waited, but there was no response from 'Boat 42'. A 7.7 mm bullet fired by one of the two intercepting Zero-sens could have knocked out the PBY's transmitter set by severing a critical transmission line, or disabling the antennas, or perhaps the radiomen themselves was hit. The radio watch in Java would receive no more signals from the patrolling PBY. The continued silence told them what they least wanted to hear. 'Boat 42' and its crew were in deep trouble over Makassar Straits, in 'Cold Turkey Lane'.

This area was heavily patrolled by Eleventh Air Fleet fighters, which were flying top cover for the invasion fleet assembling at Balikpapan. Both F1M 'Pete' floatplane fighters from the tender *Sanuki Maru* and Tainan

This memorial plaque, mounted on a wall overlooking Darwin's port, remembers the tender USS *William B Preston* and its service with PatWing 10 during the 19 February 1942 attack on Australia's northernmost city

USS WILLIAM B. PRESTON (AVD 7)

OPERATING AS A UNIT OF THE US ASIATIC FLEET, COMMANDED BY LCDR ETHERIDGE GRANT, USN, WITH VP22 SQUADRON COMMANDER LCDR FRANK O'BEIRNE, USN ABOARD, THE SHIP WAS ANCHORED IN DARWIN HARBOR ON 19 FEBRUARY 1942 TENDING SEAPLANES OF PATWINGTEN SQUADRONS VP22, VP 101, AND VP 102 WHEN JAPANESE AIR FORCES ATTACKED. STRUCK BY BOMBS WHILE UNDERWAY THE SHIP LOST TEN MEMBERS OF HER CREW AND WAS SEVERELY DAMAGED, BUT UNDER THE SKILLFUL HANDLING OF LT. LESTER O. WOOD, USN, WHO WAS ACTING COMMANDING OFFICER, WAS ABLE TO GAIN THE OPEN SEA. AFTER REPAIRS IN SYDNEY, SHE RETURNED TO WESTERN AUSTRALIA FOR CONTINUED WAR OPERATIONS. THE CATALINA SHOT DOWN THIS DATE WAS PILOTED BY LT. THOMAS H. MOORER, USN. LATER, AS A FULL ADMIRAL, HE SERVED AS CHAIRMAN, US JOINT CHIEFS OF STAFF.

THIS PLAQUE IS DEDICATED TO THE BRAVE MEN OF THE USS WILLIAM B. PRESTON AND HER ATTACHED AIRCRAFT WHO LOST THEIR LIVES 19 FEBRUARY 1942 DURING THE BATTLE OF AUSTRALIA.

Kokutai A6M Zero-sens, based ashore at a nearby captured Dutch airfield, were ever present in the area. And with a sizeable invasion fleet to protect, the IJN pilots were instructed to press home their attacks, for they knew full well that the PBY was the eyes of the defending Allied forces. If one got its sighting report off, every bomber in Java would make a beeline for the ships they were protecting. Quickly knocking the Catalina out of the sky would avoid such an attack happening. This was the fate that befell 'Boat 42'.

Lt John Robertson, and his second pilot, Chief Aviation Ordnanceman (NAP) John Long, doubtless had their hands full keeping the aeroplane in the air and headed for a cloud once it had been spotted by the Zero-sens. If the fighters had attacked from head-on, third pilot AMM1c (NAP) Z S Lewall was there with his single bow 0.30-cal machine gun. The more likely direction of the attacks was from abeam or astern the PBY, and these areas were protected by blister-mounted 0.50-cals or the tunnel 0.30-cal gun, manned by radiomen AMM2c Hans Poulsen and AOM2c Wayne Wilson, depending on who was operating the radio.

Exactly how 'Boat 42' was brought down by the Japanese fighters remains uncertain. However, drawing on the experiences of other crews in similar situations, this is how it might have happened. The first burst from the lead Zero-sen was on target, and when the Japanese pilot saw his ranging light machine gun fire hitting the PBY, he cut loose with a short burst from his 20 mm cannon. One or more shells possibly ripped through Simpson's radio compartment and knocked out the transmitter, whilst others could have penetrated the wing-to-fuselage tower, where Plane Captain ACMM Van Shelton saw his gauges shattered. These rounds would have almost certainly severed the engine controls and split fuel lines to allow the flammable liquid to drain into the hull below.

The PBY's Pratt & Whitney radials were good engines, but a ruptured lube oil line or a cannon 'slug' through a cylinder or any of a thousand other places could cause them to freeze up or fail in just seconds.

In addition, the fighters' long bursts of machine gun fire could have had a disastrous effect on the crew. Perhaps that first run cut down Wilson on the port 0.50-cal, and before Failer could pull his broken body out of the way, Poulsen, on the starboard gun, grabbed him and, amid the noise of gunfire and wind, could only point to Simpson's form crumpled over the radio key. Failer had to take over the radio and get the sighting report out. The radioman struggled forward as the PBY careened through the sky, and Poulsen turned again to his gun, lined up on the next approaching fighter, leading him carefully, and squeezed off a long burst. Maybe he got him too, as the wingman of the lead Zero-sen failed to return to base following the mission.

Chief Shelton did what he could to keep the engines alive, but the merciless gunfire was chewing up the aeroplane, and the engine controls were already ruined. So he left the tower and went aft to help Poulsen man the waist guns. Up forward, Lewall, standing up in the slipstream, was perhaps able to take careful aim at another approaching fighter, leading the tiny target and getting in a quick burst of his own.

The die was already cast, nevertheless.

Bullets from another fighter ripped through the flightdeck, hitting Chief Long in the right hand seat and killing him instantly, breaking one of Lt Robertson's arms and tearing the radio set off the bulkhead as Failer sought to get it operating again. A riddled electrical junction box sparked and gasoline spraying into the bilges from shattered fuel lines caught fire.

That is how it might have happened. That would have been all it took, and it would have been over in seconds.

The broken and blazing PBY plummeted seaward out of control and plunged into the ocean. No parachutes, no debris, just a flaming torch of burning gasoline on the water's surface where Makassar Strait had swallowed up a Catalina and its eight crewmen, topped by a tall pillar of black smoke. The victorious fighters streaked away to other battles.

Late that same afternoon back in Java, PatWing 10 waited, hopeful, ever hopeful, but with a gnawing fear of the worst. At last, there was no alternative. In the War Diary of Commander Aircraft Asiatic Fleet, there is the simple entry, 'No further word from Plane No 42'. Laconic and to the point, the staff memo recorded, 'Plane No 42 did not return to base and is presumed lost'.

The warrior's sword, however, cuts both ways, and the valiant effort of 'Boat 42's' crew was not altogether in vain. Wing Headquarters passed on their sighting report to the USAAF's 19th BG at Malang, and seven B-17s sought out and attacked the invasion convoy later that same afternoon, claiming two transports hit and sunk. Japanese records (perhaps incomplete) state that no ships were hit, and both the F1M 'Petes' and A6M Zero-sens claimed a flying-boat shot down that day. Two attacking fighters took several hits, and the A6M of Flight Petty Officer Third Class Makoto Ueda failed to return to base.

LAST PATWING 10 PBYs

PatWing 10 had performed magnificently in trying circumstances since fleeing the Philippines, gathering much intelligence on enemy movements as the invasion force steadily worked its way through the East Indies area. By the time the ill-fated Battle of the Java Sea was fought on the night of 27-28 February, only three PBY-4s remained operational. One of these was 'Boat 5', which spotted the Eastern Force heading for Java during a morning patrol on 28 February. Its crew survived an attack by Zero-sens from the Tainan *Kokutai* during the course of this mission.

Later that evening, Lt(jg) D A Campbell sortied in 'Boat 5' and witnessed much of the Battle of the Java Sea, as Combined Striking Force cruisers and destroyers vainly attempted to repulse the invasion force. The PBY crew saw the explosions and raging fires when 32 torpedoes fired by the cruisers *Nachi* and *Haguro* struck the Dutch cruisers *De Ruyter* and *Java*, although they could not identify who had been hit. Minutes later they flew over the blacked-out transports of the invasion convoy, and this sighting was reported to base by 'Boat 5's' radioman.

Finally, some while later, they passed low over two darkened warships steering west. Again unable to identify the shadows, the PBY crew had almost certainly seen the cruisers HMAS *Perth* and USS *Houston* withdrawing. Both vessels would be sunk by four Japanese cruisers and nine destroyers the following night with the loss of 1008 Allied sailors.

The invasion of Java on 29 February signalled the end of PBY operations in the East Indies, the Allied command in the region being dissolved and remaining US naval forces evacuated to Australia. The British had surrendered Singapore on 15 February, and the Dutch would

'Airedale' sailors RM3c Larry Katz (left) and RM2c Vernard Nichols enjoy a spot of liberty in Honolulu in 1941. Katz deployed in April 1942 to Australia with PatWing 10's VP-21, while Nichols went pre-war to VP-102 in the Philippines and was eventually evacuated from Java in March in a submarine (*Larry Katz*)

Lt(jg) Thomas F Pollock, who commanded the lead *Gridiron* PBY sent to Corregidor at the end of April 1942, is seen here posing with VP-102's 'Boat 5', PBY-4 BuNo 1216, at Olongapo in early 1940 prior to it receiving its camouflage paint scheme. VP-102 did not use the hull waterline stripe as employed by VP-21 and other PatWing squadrons at the time. Pollock ended his naval career with the rank of captain (*T F Pollock*)

RM3c Windsor 'Ned' Kelly and RM2c Harold Donahue were also veterans of the heroic *Gridiron* flight. This photograph was taken in Perth in May 1942 (*Larry Katz*)

follow suit on Java on 8 March, thus concluding the Japanese thrust into the rich 'Southern Resources Area' that had been a major objective when they commenced hostilities in the Pacific on 7 December 1941.

On 2 March, 'Boat 5', now commanded by Lt(jg) Charlie Hoffman, transported Admiral William A Glassford and other senior US Navy personnel to Australia to regroup and continue the fight. The aircraft headed for the seaplane tender USS *Childs*, anchored in Exmouth Gulf off the coast of Western Australia. Here, Lt(jg) Thomas F Pollock (ex-VP-102) took over the PBY and flew Glassford, PatWing 10 CO Cdr Wagner and a number of other key personnel south to Perth, where they arrived just after dawn on 3 March. British Rear Admiral A F E Palliser also departed Java on another PatWing 10 PBY ('Boat 46') on 2 March, and he arrived in Perth at the same time as Glassford and his staff.

In an effort to boost the Asiatic Fleet's meagre PBY resources (three Catalinas) in Western Australia, Commander-in-Chief Pacific Fleet (CINCPAC) ordered VP-21 and its 12 PBY-5s from Pearl Harbor to Perth in April 1942. PatWing 10's VP-101 would now have sufficient strength in numbers to declare itself fully operational once again.

One of the first things the unit did following VP-21's arrival was to commence Operation *Gridiron* in support of beleaguered forces in the Philippines. Bataan had surrendered on 9 April, and the situation on Corregidor was growing progressively worse with each passing day. PatWing 10 duly sent ex-VP-21 PBY-5s, 'Boat 1', flown by Lt(jg) Tom Pollock, and 'Boat 7', with Lt(jg) Leroy Deede at the controls, north in a daring effort to help re-supply operations to the embattled island. They loaded ammunition and medicines in Darwin and then headed up to Lake Lanao, in the Mindanao highlands, which was still in American control. The PBYs then flew the final leg to Corregidor, landing in the ocean just south of the island in the darkness on the night of 29-30 April.

Once on the water, the crews unloaded their freight into boats and took aboard selected evacuees, before quickly heading off again. They initially returned to Lake Lanao for fuel, and when the the PBYs headed out the next morning, 'Boat 1' grounded on a submerged rock and could not take-off. Pollock signalled to Deede to go on without him. With the Philippines collapsing about his ears, and being a veteran of Bataan himself, this was not one of Tom Pollock's happier wartime memories.

Good fortune and a supreme effort by dedicated and creative people eventually made the PBY sufficiently water tight to allow it to take off, and the aircraft made it to Darwin and then Perth without further trouble. Upon landing in the latter city's Swan River, Pollock grounded 'Boat 1' on the sandy shore before it sank. A veteran of the attack on Pearl Harbor, PBY-5 BuNo 2446 had come through with flying colours.

Corregidor eventually surrendered on 6 May 1942, and amongst the many thousands of Americans and Filipinos that went into captivity there were some 200 PatWing 10 men – both flight crews and shore party.

And thus, as the dust settled for the moment, PatWing 10, with one PBY-4 ('Boat 5' BuNo 1216) and two PBY-5s ('Boat 10' BuNo 2292 and 'Boat 46'), plus 12 retreaded Pearl Harbor veterans, established a new home on the Swan River in Perth. Thereafter, all PBY base movements would be northward, toward Tokyo.

CORAL SEA, MIDWAY AND THE ALEUTIANS

In the immediate wake of the devastating attacks on Pearl Harbor and the Philippines, the US Navy made one of its priorities the restoration of the 'Eyes of the Fleet' – the return of VP squadrons to full strength so at to allow the Pacific Fleet to see what lay over the horizon. It needed to know whether invasion transports were heading for Hawaii or even possibly the west coast of the USA. Flying in squadrons from the east coast to boost PatWing numbers was only a short term solution.

The Consolidated plant in San Diego responded quickly to the urgent call put out by the US Navy for more Catalinas, delivering 39 new PBY-5/5As in December – 15 of the amphibians were issued to VP-91 at Alameda. Deliveries from the plant rose sharply at this point, and then steadied thereafter. These aircraft were sorely needed in the frontline, as many Pacific Fleet units still had less than a full complement, while some PBYs went to Atlantic Fleet squadrons.

Besides the effort to get VP-22 sent from Hawaii to the Philippines in early January 1942, VP-23 also despatched its new PBY-5s on patrols westward from Ford and established a small detachment on Canton Island, which was part of the Gilbert Islands chain in the South Pacific. Very quickly, increasing enemy activity would draw VP-23 still further south. VP-14 was sent to the South Pacific from Kaneohe on 7 February to help share VP-23's operational burden, the unit taking a mix of new PBYs and aircraft borrowed from VP-11. Once in-theatre, VP-23 began mounting patrols from Suva, Fiji and Noumea, with the recently-repaired seaplane tender USS *Curtiss* sailing down from Hawaii to help support operations.

Back at home, new PBY-5s went to VP-43 in San Diego, VP-71 at Alameda as it worked up and, in April, to VP-11, thus returning the PatWing 2 squadron to full readiness. VP-44 in San Diego received new PBY-5A amphibians, with others going to PatWing 4's VP-41 and VP-42. The latter units used them to patrol the northern Pacific from the new Naval Air Facility at Tongue Point, in Oregon, from NAS Seattle and from the harbour at Naval Station Kodiak, in Alaska.

A PBY-5 prepares to depart NAS Kaneohe, having been tractored down the seaplane ramp in its beaching gear. Pali is in the background and Pearl Harbor is on the other side of the mountain range. The red and white rudder markings date this photograph as having been taken pre-May 1942 (*US Navy*)

VP-24 received PBY-5As in April, and on 1 May PatWing 8 was established at Alameda with three new squadrons – VP-53, VP-61 and VP-62 – all equipped with the PBY-5A.

Backed by the might of the US aviation industry, which was now achieving wartime production rates, VP squadrons in the Pacific were putting the lows of Pearl Harbor behind them and even extending their reach southward to Australia. Strategically, the 'hold-the-line' mentality that had gripped US forces in the region was changed with the arrival of new aircraft and naval vessels. The first real example of striking back occurred when 16 USAAF B-25s launched from the brand new carrier USS *Hornet* and attacked Japan on 18 April 1942.

Sailors conduct routine maintenance on the engines of a PBY at NAS Pearl Harbor in the weeks following the raid on the base (*US Navy*)

While the PBYs played no direct part in this operation, the Doolittle raid dramatically changed the way the Japanese viewed their own position. Indeed, the shaken leadership in Tokyo acceded to Admiral Isoroku Yamamoto's demand to take Midway Island and force the Pacific Fleet into a decisive engagement. Therewith was set in motion a very great series of events in which PBYs *did* play a crucial role.

CORAL SEA AND MIDWAY

The US Navy's codebreakers (the Combat Intelligence Unit at Pearl Harbor, later known as FRUPAC, Fleet Radio Unit Pacific) had been listening to Japanese military radio signals since before the raid on Pearl Harbor, producing communications intelligence (COMINT) on future campaigns. The decoding of increasingly larger chunks of the Imperial Japanese Navy's operational message traffic indicated that preparations were underway for two major offensives. The first of these would see the enemy attempt to seize Port Moresby, in New Guinea, and thus secure a base from which to threaten Australia. CINCPAC Admiral Chester W Nimitz, based in Pearl Harbor, knew that he had to stop this happening.

Since January, VP-23's small det had been patrolling from Fiji and other nearby islands as the PBY made its combat debut in the South Pacific. On 3 March USS *Tangier* relieved USS *Curtiss* as the seaplane tender in residence in Noumea. By then a detachment from VP-14 had also arrived in-theatre, and it was running patrols north from Noumea out to a distance of some 700 miles. The operational burden placed on

VP-14 PBY-5 '11-P-7', borrowed from VP-11 for the unit's South Pacific deployment, is hoisted aboard USS *Tangier* for maintenance work at Noumea in early 1942. As a recognition feature, naval aircraft in the Pacific wore 13 alternate red and white rudder stripes between December 1941 and May 1942, after which they were ordered to be removed (*US Navy*)

these small detachments was proving too great, however, so the commander of PatWing 2 despatched VP-71 to Noumea on 1 May. Amongst the aircraft sent south by the unit from Kaneohe was PBY-5 BuNo 2327, which was the first PBY in the Pacific Fleet to be equipped with radar. A VP-72 detachment, and the seaplane tender USS *Wright*, would soon follow them.

Rear Admiral Frank Jack Fletcher's Pacific Fleet Task Force 11, centred around the carrier USS *Yorktown*, was already present in the South Pacific, and the vessel's radiomen routinely listened to the PBY circuit for their scouting reports. Correctly reading the situation with the aid of reports from his codebreakers, CINCPAC sent Rear Admiral Aubrey Fitch's TF-17, which boasted the carrier USS *Lexington* (TF 17), to add more muscle to Fletcher's force. Nimitz gambled that the Japanese would not expect two American carriers to be present in the area in such force.

An aerial view of Midway Islands, in the central Pacific – the scene of one of World War 2's most pivotal battles. Eastern Island, in the foreground, was dominated by an airfield for land-based aircraft, while Sand Island, in the distance, was home to a seaplane base

Each carrier used its own SBD scouting squadrons to search out as far as 300 miles from the task force, concentrating on the sectors thought to be most likely exploited by the enemy. These aircraft were supported by the VP squadrons in the area, which typically could cover greater distances from their shore bases.

The IJN's 5th Carrier Division and US naval forces duly clashed head on during the strategically crucial Battle of the Coral Sea, which was fought between 4-8 May. Although *Lexington* was sunk during the engagement, the battle had stopped the enemy thrust towards Australia. Indeed, the expansion of the Japanese Empire was now very near reaching its zenith. Historically, too, the battle was significant, as it was fought entirely by aircraft. Note a single shot was exchanged between surface ships.

Having enjoyed success at Coral Sea, Admiral Nimitz's confidence in his codebreakers soared. In the basement of the 14th Naval District headquarters building in the Pearl Harbor Navy Yard they burned the

Also present at Pearl Harbor, seaplane tender USS *Tangier* was commissioned into the US Navy in July 1940. A veteran of numerous engagements throughout the Pacific campaign, the vessel is seen here – with a PBY on its afterdeck – whilst moored off Noumea, in New Caledonia, in early 1942. An OS2U Kingfisher sits on the deck to the right of the Catalina (*US Navy*)

midnight oil reading more and more intercepts, but only fragments of the emerging operation order for the next big thrust were being deciphered. Nimitz immediately recalled Admiral Halsey with *Enterprise* and *Hornet*, as well as Fletcher in *Yorktown*, from the South Pacific and speculatively sent them towards Midway Island.

Thanks to further deciphering of Japanese JN25 codes, CINCPAC's hunch that Midway was the next target on the enemy's agenda was confirmed. Nimitz guessed that this was Yamamoto's bid for a major fleet action with the Americans, and he decided that he would set a trap of his own. He packed the island with all the aerial resources available, including 15 PBY-5As (six from VP-24, seven from VP-44 and three from VP-51) based ashore on nearby Eastern Island and 14 PBY-5s from VP-23 at the seaplane facility on Sand Island. In addition, VP-91 was deployed to Barking Sands, on Kauai, in order to cover the ocean between Hawaii and Midway.

COMINT notwithstanding, it remained for the 'eyes of the fleet' to actually locate the approaching enemy carriers. Midway PBYs duly covered the vast tract of the Pacific Ocean 200 degrees west through 020 degrees north of their island bases. The longer-ranged PBY-5s of VP-23 patrolled the northern sectors in their search for the Japanese carrier force, while the PBY-5As scoured the seas west of Midway looking for the invasion transports.

VP-44's Ens Jack 'Jewel' Reid and his crew, flying '44-P-4' (call sign '8V55'), were the first to spot the enemy, on bearing 262 degrees, some 700 miles from Midway just before noon on 3 June. They radioed back to base to tell them that they had seen the 'main body', but what they had actually sighted was the invasion force of transports and escorts, not the carriers.

That sighting resulted in several attacks being made on the Japanese vessels, including the first ever night torpedo run made by PBYs. Lt 'Red' Richards of VP-44 led the attack in Ens Chas Hibberd's '24-P-12', leading Lt(jg) Douglas C Davis in '24-P-7', Ens Gaylord Probst in '24-P-11' and Ens Allan Rothenburg in '51-P-5'. One torpedo hit a tanker, but the force sailed on.

Although Admiral Nimitz was happy that the invasion fleet had been spotted, what he really wanted was the location of the carrier striking force. Admiral Raymond Spruance's *Enterprise* and *Hornet*, along with Admiral Fletcher in *Yorktown*, were ordered to redouble their efforts to find the four Japanese carriers, as were the PBYs on Midway.

Responding to this call, before dawn on 4 June, VP-23 launched 11 PBY-5s on 15 sector patrols covering the anticipated direction from which COMINT indicated the Japanese carriers would come. The sector assigned to Lt Howard Ady (operating with the call sign '4V58'), centred on 315 degrees,

Bombs are loaded onto a VP-91 PBY-5A at NAS Midway in June 1942, sailors above and below the wing coordinating the shackling of the 500-lb weapons. Note the torpedo rack to the left of the bombs (*Dave's Warbirds*)

Midway's night torpedo attack pilots, Lt (jg) Douglas C Davis (a Dutch East Indies PBY veteran) of VP-24, who flew '24-P-7', Ens Allan Rothenburg in '51-P-5', Lt William L Richards, XO of VP-44 and mission commander in Lt (jg) Charles P Hibberd's '24-P-12', and Ens Gaylord D Probst in '24-P-11'

The VP-23 crew that spotted the Midway Occupation Force pose in front of their PBY-5A. They are, standing, from left to right, AMM2c R J Derouin, Chief Aviation Radioman Francis Musser, second pilot Ens Hardeman, Ens Reid, sat on the wheel, and Ens R A Swan (navigator). Kneeling, from left to right, are third pilot AMM1c (NAP) J F Gammell and AMM3cs J Goovers and P A Fitzpatrick

and he would fly outbound on the right, dogleg to the left and then fly back down the left side of the sector.

At 0510 hrs Ady's crew spotted a Japanese scout aircraft from one of the carriers heading for Midway, and then at 0530 hrs the carrier striking force was located by the PBY crew. Seconds later, Ady's radioman quickly began keying out their contact report – 'Enemy carriers!' The PBYs had flushed out the quarry.

The *Kido Butai* was in the process of launching its morning strike on Midway when discovered. Lt(jg) William Chase, patrolling the adjoining sector, radioed Sand Island at 0544 hrs with the message 'Many aeroplanes heading for Midway'. This signal triggered the launch of every flyable aircraft on the island that could get airborne, either to attack the carriers or get out of the way. Meanwhile, Ady and his crew got a better view of what was below them, allowing them to amplify their sighting at 0552 hrs.

Aboard the American carriers, Admiral Spruance in *Enterprise* was fully prepared to strike at the Japanese carriers, and was just waiting for the right information that would allow his air wing to pounce. These first hurried reports from the patrolling PBYs were frustratingly incomplete, however, even though the Japanese vessels had appeared precisely where COMINT had said they would. Then came Ady's 0552 hrs signal – 'From "4V58". Two carriers and battleships, bearing 320, distance 180, course 135, speed 25'. The PBY crew had seen only two of the 'flattops', but that was enough.

With this information in hand, and knowing his carrier groups would be attacking at extreme range (the Japanese fleet was actually more than 200 miles away from the US carriers), Admiral Spruance gave the order to launch aircraft at 0700 hrs. This directive was relayed to *Enterprise* and *Hornet* via signalman's light at 0638 hrs.

By then Marine Corps, US Navy and USAAF aircraft from Midway Island were already on their way to attack the Japanese carriers. A number of PBY crewmen also took part in this strike, as the island-based VT-8 detachment, flying six brand new Grumman TBF-1 Avenger torpedo-bombers, needed assistance with navigation and crewing. Four PBY men stepped forward to assist, namely Enss Joseph M Hissem and Jack Wilkes from VP-24, who would navigate for the formation, and turret gunners AMM1 William M Coffee and AOM3 Lyonel J Ogeren from VP-44. Only one TBF returned from the mission, and all four Catalina crewmen perished.

After the intensity of the morning's air battles the PBYs still had work to do rescuing aircrew from downed aircraft or sailors from sunken ships. The effort to pull from the water any survivors started even before the last shots had been fired in anger. The Catalinas were naturally the

A PBY-5 is rearmed on the apron at NAS Midway in the summer of 1942. Sailors used portable winches on top of the wings to lift ordnance via cables fed through tubes in the wings to the bombs themselves, the latter positioned on trucks parked beneath the Catalina's underwing racks. A PBY could carry two 500-lb bombs or a 2000-lb aerial torpedo under each wing, with a reduction in fuel load and, therefore, range, to meet many varied mission requirements (*Dave's Warbirds*)

The seaplane hangar on Sand Island was attacked on 7 December 1941 and again on 4 June 1942, being badly damaged on both occasions. This photograph was taken shortly after it had been bombed by IJN aircraft on the latter date

most effective aircraft in-theatre for this task, and with attacks on the carriers still in progress, VP-23's Lt(jg) Harold W Lough spotted and pulled from the water a VB-8 SBD dive-bomber crew from *Hornet*.

The very next day, with the balance of the battle still unclear to many, VP-44's Lt(jg) Samuel Cole and crew found Ens George Gay in the water, and their first question to the rescued pilot was whether he had seen any Zeros around recently. Ens Gay was the sole survivor of *Hornet's* ill-fated TBD Devastator unit VT-8. Elsewhere, the VP-91 Catalina flown by Lt Samuel Ogden found Marine Corps aviators Capt Richard L Blain and his gunner PFC Gordon R McFeely from Midway-based SBD unit VMSB-241. Finally, Lt(jg) Stewart Cooper and his crew in a VP-51 PBY recovered Capt Glen H Cramer and his B-26 crewmen from the USAAF's 72nd BS.

As late as 21 June, the Catalinas were still out looking for survivors, and VP-24's Lt(jg) John L White and crew duly landed in the ocean to take aboard Machinist Arthur W Winchell and his gunner, ARM3 Douglas M Cossitt, of *Yorktown's* VT-6 on this date.

More than 200 aircrew from at least 18 different Marine Corps, US Navy and USAAF squadrons went into the water during the day-long battles of 4 June. Between that date and 21 June, 12 PBYs made no fewer than 13 landings at sea to recover 41 American aircrew. The rest sadly perished.

The PBY squadrons' work did not go unopposed either, with F1M2 'Petes' launched from vessels protecting the invasion convoy intercepting several PBYs and shooting down Lt(jg) Whiteman's '44-P-12' (BuNo 04975) on 4 June. The seaplane fighters killed Whiteman and Ens Walter Mosely, sat in the right hand seat. A survivor from this engagement was Ens Lee McCleary, who took over as the aircraft's co-pilot as the 'Petes' made one pass after another until his aeroplane refused to fly any more. Many years later he told the author;

'The floatplane fighters came sliding in on our starboard wing and let fly with machine gun and cannon. The aircraft was filled with flying rivets and metal torn from the PBY's outer skin, as the enemy fighters' fire had blown all the rivets and metal along the upper fuselage ribs. With the wing tower shredded, the engines out and most of the crew dead or mortally wounded, we simply crashed into the sea. I was the only one lucky enough to survive from the front section of the aeroplane.'

Late in the afternoon of 6 June, and at the outer limit of their search pattern, VP-23's Lt(jg) Norman K Brady and crew elected to push on a little further before doglegging to the left, and in doing so spotted a raft below them. Landing on the ocean, they rescued Enss McCleary and Jack H Camp, although the latter was so badly wounded that he later died, and three men from the rear section of the PBY, AMM1 Virgil R Marsh, AMM2 John C Weeks and AOM2 Philip L Fulghum.

Of course, the US carrier force, supported by Midway-based aircraft, soundly beat the *Kido Butai* between 4 and 6 June in what ultimately proved to be the Pacific War's pivotal battle. Admiral Spruance had trusted the PBYs to find the Japanese carriers, and they had certainly not let him down.

THE ALEUTIANS

As part of the Midway battle plan, Japanese forces landed on 3 June on the islands of Kiska and Attu at the near-westernmost extremity of the Aleutians, some 700 miles from the Unalaskan port town of Dutch Harbor. They hoped to draw American attention away from bigger things further south, and thus catch them off guard. For both sides, the bitter, unpredictable weather in the northern Pacific proved to be by far the greatest adversary.

For PatWing 4, sent word of the invasion by CINCPAC, its 20 PBYs on Kodiak (supported by three tenders) had been battling with the weather well before the Japanese arrived. In April, VP-42's PBY-5A BuNo 7286 had crashed whilst attempting to take-off from Dutch Harbor when the strong headwind shifted sharply after the pilot was committed and the flying-boat could not get off in the downwind conditions. Within two weeks, BuNo 7275, piloted by Ens E R Winters and crew, failed to return from a patrol in poor weather that suddenly turned very much worse within minutes of the PBY's departure. No trace of the aircraft, or its crew, was ever found.

By early June VP-42 had four PBY-5As aboard the tender USS *Gillis* in Dutch Harbor, four on USS *Casco* in Cold Bay and four more in Sand Point aboard USS *Williamson*. VP-41 was similarly deployed.

On 2 June '42-P-4' went down after departing Sand Point, although its crew was rescued by *Gillis*.

Unperturbed by these losses, both units sent out patrols on the 3rd that were expected to encounter the enemy, and during one of these flights, the PBY flown by VP-41's Lt(jg) Jean Cusick and crew just disappeared. Elsewhere, south of Dutch Harbor, Lt(jg) L D Campbell in '42-P-6' found one of the two carriers of the Second Carrier Strike Force that were supporting the landings. The PBY was badly shot up by Zero-sens and forced to ditch before the crew could send a sighting report back to base. The crew scrambled into their liferaft in frigid waters and were fortunate enough to be rescued by the US Coast Guard Cutter *Nemaha* just 30 minutes later.

Two other aerial clashes also took place on the 3rd, with Lt Boyle – in '42-P-11' – fighting off a pair of F1Ms and returning to base with battle damage, while carrier fighters engaged Ens Hildebrant's PBY over Dutch Harbor. The crew were fortunate enough to escape with their lives by flying their aircraft into the gathering overcast.

On 4 June, Lt(jg) Freerks in '41-P-11' spotted both carriers 240 miles southwest of Otter Point. Ens Mitchell in '42-P-4' almost certainly saw them as well, but fighters patrolling ahead of the task force sent the PBY down in flames. Later that day Lt C E Perkins in '42-P-5' (BuNo 7281) reported carriers just 160 miles southwest of Otter Point, but when anti-aircraft fire from the fleet knocked out one of the PBY's engines, he jettisoned his bombs and headed back to base.

This photograph, published in a wartime Japanese magazine, purports to show a PatWing 4 PBY-5 shortly after it was 'winged' by flak during a bombing run on Japanese forces in Kiska harbour in June 1942. Note the trail of smoke streaming from the aircraft's port engine (*Robert Bergstrom*)

A second PBY was lost on the 4th when Lt(jg) Gene Stockstill, in '42-P-11', departed from Cold Bay to relieve Freerks and his crew and disappeared. Wreckage of the aircraft lay undiscovered for 60 years high up on the Kiska volcano.

The following day, VP-41's Lt William Thies returned from his patrol to report an aircraft down on Akutan Island – an A6M2 Zero-sen, which was subsequently recovered and became the first example of the legendary Mitsubishi fighter to be test flown by the Americans.

Having bombed Dutch Harbor on the 4th, the Japanese task force then appeared to withdraw from the area. This lull in the action allowed PatWing 4 to provide an action report to CINCPAC and order VP-43 forward from Seattle. On 9 June, the first four PBY-5As from this unit rendezvoused with *Gillis*, which had by now headed west in the Aleutians to Nazan Bay, off the island of Atka. The rest of the squadron soon followed, bringing with it detachments from VP-51 and newly-formed VP-61 and VP-62.

At this time, all PBY crews in PatWing 4 were cheered by the message sent to them by the US Navy's Commander-in-Chief, Admiral Ernie King, who handed out such praise sparingly.

On 10 June VP-41's Lt Litsey and crew, who were patrolling in their PBY some 400 miles west of *Gillis*, spotted unidentified ships in Kiska harbour. This proved that the Japanese had not withdrawn as first hoped. PatWing 4 immediately ordered his units to bomb the enemy out of Kiska. From Sand Point, '42-P-7', '42-P-8' and '42-P-12' flew to Dutch Harbor to be loaded with ordnance so as to implement the 'Kiska Blitz' directive. Every PBY that could fly got a bomb and made a run.

That same day, Machinist Leland Davis, flying '43-P-10' depth-charged a submarine in the area.

The shuttle attacks on Kiska continued, even when the target was socked in – the PBY crews would estimate when to drop their bombs through the overcast by working their aim point distances off the tall Kiska volcano.

On the morning of 12 June, Lt(jg) Ed Bergstrom, in BuNo 7283, flew from Dutch Harbor to Kiska to drop his ordnance and then returned to *Gillis* in Nazan Bay, by which time the PBY had been in the air for 14.7 hours. It then headed from Atka to Unmak that afternoon, and on to Cold Bay the following day. Flights over such distances, often in poor weather, were physically demanding, and the anti-aircraft fire that greeted the PBYs over their targets seemed thick and accurate. Despite their best efforts, PatWing 4 achieved only meagre results in terms of damage done due to the PBY's modest bomb load.

Remarkably, only a single PBY was lost during the 'Blitz' when Machinist Davis, on his second or third mission to Kiska, dived on his target and never pulled out of the dive. On a more positive note, a Catalina strafed four H6K 'Mavis' flying-boats spotted on the water off the island and set two of them alight.

US Navy Commander-in-Chief Admiral Ernie King sent this message to PatWing 4 following its efforts of 8 June as part of the 'Kiska Blitz' (*Robert Bergstrom*)

CLASSIFIED — U.S. NAVAL COMMUNICATION SERVICE — COMMANDER-IN-CHIEF U. S. PACIFIC FLEET — INCOMING

CONFIDENTIAL 081245 PRIORITY

COMINCH MOST FULLY AND HEARTILY CONCURS IN CINCPAC 072145 XX CARRY ON AND HOLD ON AND WE WILL CASH IN ON THE SPLENDID WORK YOUR GALLANT FORCES HAVE DONE IN THE FACE OF THE ENEMY DESPITE THE HELLISH WEATHER

REF: THE BATTLE OF MIDWAY HAS NOT LESSENED MY CLOSE FOLLOWING OF YOUR SPLENDID EFFORTS X YOUR TIRELESS PERSISTENCE YOUR COURAGE AND THE BULLDOG GRIP YOU HAVE EPT [sic] ON THE ENEMY IN SNOW RAIN AND FOG HAVE AROUSED MY ADMIRATION X

DATE 8 JUNE '42 CRYPTO GROUP 133C CBO REH

ORIGINATOR: COMINCH 081245

ACTION: COMALSEC CTF 8 CPW 4

INFORMATION: CINCPAC COMNOWESEAFRON [sic]

Shortly after this mission, a Japanese floatplane from one of the enemy's cruisers found *Gillis* off Atka, thus rendering its position there untenable. This signalled an end to the 'Blitz' on 13 June, by which time the PBYs had exhausted their stock of bombs in any case. Although having inflicted little damage on the Japanese invasion force, the ferocity and courage shown by the American airmen in attacking a considerably larger foe had impressed the Japanese, and they shifted to a more defensive posture following the offensive. PatWing 4 continued its aggressive patrolling so as to keep abreast of the enemy's movements in the Aleutians.

Amongst the pilots conducting these daily reconnaissance missions was Ens Julius Raven, who, on 24 June, in PBY-5A BuNo 04980, was overflying the previously abandoned Amchitka Island when he was surprised to find a group of men gathered at the settlement at Constantine Harbor. As the PBY made two passes over a clutch of huts, the strangers began signalling to the crew with an Aldis lamp, and then laid out a US ensign on the beach. The men turned out to be the crew of the shipwrecked US submarine S 27, who were very happy to be found. The PBY's young signalman striker, S2c George Harold, remembered the Catalina's signal in response – 'Will send position. Will land'.

Like the PBYs, the submarine had also been scouting the location of the Japanese, and rounding the southern end of Amchitka, headed for Kiska, the vessel had surfaced during the midwatch on 19 June in order to recharge its batteries. Impenetrable fog and unpredictable currents had subsequently swept the submarine closer to the island, and it grounded on the rocks off St Makarius Point. Efforts to pull S 27 off were unsuccessful, and the captain ordered the vessel stripped of survival gear and his crew ashore at first light the following morning.

The hike over to Constantine Harbor caused the sailors less anxiety than knowing that the Japanese were ashore on Kiska, just a stone's throw west of them across open water. The appearance of a US Navy PBY was literally 'Christmas in June' for them, and Raven's aircraft lifted out a first group, and three more Catalinas followed the next day to extract the entire crew to Dutch Harbor.

Not all missions ended so positively, however, with the weather often having the final say in the fate of a PBY and its crew. On 30 July, following a long patrol, Lt(jg) David A Brough and his crew in '42-P-10' (BuNo 7291) crashed in rough seas attempting to land at Cold Bay – only the three petty officers back aft survived. Then, on 8 August, Lt(jg) Raven and his crew were returning to Dutch Harbor after sunset following yet another rescue mission at sea when they were radioed a message advising them of very bad weather at their destination. Instructed to head for Unmak instead, the PBY clearly had not received the first transmission for the crew reported their arrival off Dutch Harbor at 2340 hrs. Asking for guidance through the blackness so that they could land, shortly after midnight the radio signals ceased and the PBY disappeared with all hands.

Such losses were, sadly, all too common in the Aleutians, where the weather was often a more deadly enemy than the Japanese.

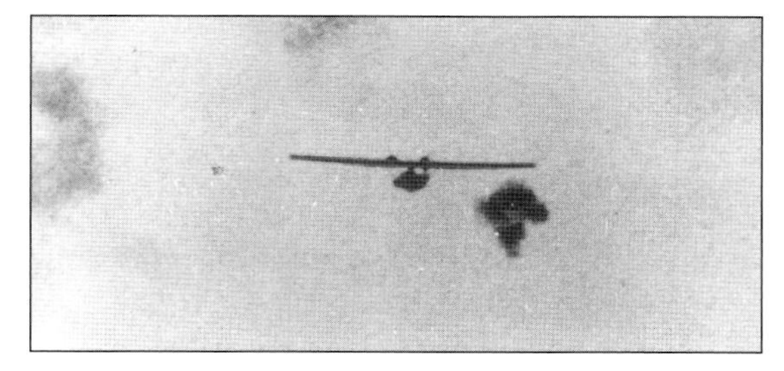

The 'Kiska Blitz' from the 'other side of the hill'. Flak gunners try to bring down a PatWing 4 PBY as it attacks IJN vessels in Kiska harbor in June 1942. This still is from a captured Japanese filmstrip (*Robert Bergstrom*)

MORE FIGHTING IN 1942

Despite Consolidated's best efforts, by mid-1942 there were still not enough PBYs to go around in the Pacific Fleet. This meant that none of the 15 VP units in-theatre had their full complement of aircraft. Still, the PatWings got on with the job without much in the way of back up from the USA.

Following the Battle of Midway, the Pacific Fleet's primary focus in the second half of 1942 was supporting operations in the Southwest Pacific's Solomon Islands chain, and specifically the island of Guadalcanal. In mid-April the Japanese invaded the southern Solomons as far as Guadalcanal, and the enemy's advances in this region had provided the impetus for the Battle of the Coral Sea. In the weeks following the large-scale naval clashes in April and May, PBYs operating from Noumea and Espiritu Santo had continued to watch developments in the Solomons.

VP-23's PBYs had initially bombed Japanese forces in the region on 25 July, with VP-71's Catalinas conducting a follow-up mission four days later. These attacks came at around the same time that COMINT decrypters managed to decipher a signal that suggested an airfield was being built on one of the Solomon islands. A USAAF B-17 from Townsville, in Australia, confirmed its presence on Guadalcanal with photography, and Noumea-based PBYs followed up with a scouting mission to the island, some 700 miles to the north of their base. Photographs from these missions clearly showed the outline of an airfield emerging from the dense jungle that covered Guadalcanal. Japanese bombers flying from this base would pose a serious threat to the Hawaii-Australia defensive line observed by the Allies in the region.

Fortuitously, the amphibiously-trained 1st Marine Division was then embarked and heading for a different South Pacific target, and, with the latest intelligence information in hand, Admiral Nimitz simply redirected the force to Guadalcanal. A major question in the minds of those in command was how, and in what manner, the Japanese would retaliate. Detecting their response would be the job of the PatWing units in the region, the PBY crews being responsible for reconnoitring the enemy's movements as early as possible.

To support this crucial mission, the brand new small seaplane tender USS *Mackinac* was sent north to Malaita Island, northeast of Guadalcanal. This remote anchorage would be home for VP-23's detachment of nine PBYs as they scouted the ocean to the north in the direction of the enemy stronghold of Rabaul on the northern tip of the island of New Britain, northeast of New Guinea.

On the morning of 7 August 1942, the heavy cruiser USS *Quincey* and two other vessels of a similar size opened fire on the unsuspecting

Japanese forces on Guadalcanal. Shortly thereafter the 1st Marine Division went ashore to stay.

Aside from VP-23's detachment flying long patrols in search of an enemy response to the invasion of Guadalacanal, many other units also worked in support of this pivotal campaign. Vice Admiral John S McCain, as Commander Aircraft South Pacific Force (COMAIR-SOPAC), had hoisted his flag in the tender USS *Curtiss* at Noumea and promptly ordered the vessel forward on 11 August to Espiritu Santo so that the PBYs under his control were closer to the scene of action. This move saw VP-14's two-PBY detachment, VP-72 det's three Catalinas and VP-11's 16 PBY-5s (which had been operating with the tender USS *McFarland* from Tongatabu) all brought together in Espiritu Santo with *Curtiss*, which was also supporting the admiral's PBY-5A.

Built as a *Clemson* class destroyer and commissioned into the US Navy's Atlantic Fleet in September 1920, USS *McFarland* became a seaplane tender in August 1940. Assigned to the Pacific Fleet in Hawaii, the vessel was sailing off Maui when Pearl Harbor was attacked. Sent to the South Pacific in June 1942, *McFarland* played an active part in the Solomons campaign despite the vessel's crowded deck space. On 16 October 1942, while off Guadalcanal unloading cargo and embarking combat casualties, the ship was attacked by Japanese dive-bombers. One bomb hit a gasoline barge tied up alongside and others hit or near-missed *McFarland*. The US Navy recognised the crew's performance in saving their vessel under very difficult conditions with a Presidential Unit Citation – the first one ever awarded to a ship. *McFarland* eventually returned to San Francisco to be repaired, and spent the rest of the war sailing out of San Diego (*US Navy*)

Ashore on Tulagi, and on the nearby islands of Gavutu-Tanamboga and Florida, the Japanese defended with determination, but across the sound on Guadalcanal, where there had been insufficient time to prepare defences, the Marines simply walked up the beaches and had the entire near-complete airfield firmly in their control by the second day. Still, the struggle for what the Marines soon referred to simply as 'the Canal' would rage fiercely and hang in the balance for many desperate weeks to come.

The very basic Australian seaplane facility that had existed on Gavutu-Tanamboga prior to the Japanese invasion had been enlarged by the enemy since its seizure some weeks earlier. When VP-11's Lt Jack Coley briefed aboard *Curtiss* on the morning of 7 August prior to his long patrol down the 'Slot' between islands in the Solomon chain, he was told that that seaplane facility on Gavutu-Tanamboga would be securely in Marine Corps hands by the time his mission had ended. Coley was advised to recover there in order to replenish his fuel and ammunition, before heading back to *Curtiss*.

Although the Marines would indeed eventually prevail, the Tulagi/Gavutu/Halavo area was stoutly defended, and it required several days of hard fighting to clean out the Japanese. No one informed Lt(jg) Coley about this, however, and he brought his PBY in for a perfect full stall landing on the sheltered waters at dusk. The flying-boat was quickly surrounded by surprised, and very heavily armed, Marines who were not at all sure of the PBY's identity. Fortunately, the sailors and Marines 'got acquainted' without gunfire being exchanged, but the ranking officer briefing Coley recommended that he get away at first light, as the position was not at all safe for a large flying-boat on the water.

US Navy SeaBees would soon enlarge the base, and also create a major seaplane support facility at nearby Halavo Point, but August 1942 was still too early for PBYs to be operating from the waters in this part of the Solomon Islands. Nevertheless, the first aircraft to land in-theatre after the Marines had come ashore was a PBY!

As this mission clearly showed, all the Catalina crews were keen to support the first US amphibious assault operation of the war by supplying the troops on the ground with any and all information relating to enemy movements. However, west of the Solomons chain was the dividing line between theatres – Southwest Pacific to the left and South Pacific to the right. Scouting in the western sector was the responsibility of a separate force of land-based Royal Australian Air Force (RAAF) and USAAF aircraft.

At midday on 7 August, a land-based RAAF Hudson bomber from Southwest Pacific Command spotted a powerful force consisting of seven Japanese cruisers and a destroyer steering south for the Solomons from Rabaul. Its sighting report somehow got delayed after it was sent, and the devastatingly one-sided Battle of Savo Island (the small island which lay just north of Guadalcanal) was fought on the night of 7/8 August. Four of the five Allied cruisers attacked by the enemy force were quickly sunk in an action which lasted barely 30 minutes.

By then most of the Marines had already been sent ashore, but great quantities of essential supplies were yet to be unloaded, and with their cruiser guardians now sunk, the only partially unloaded transports were defenceless and exposed to further enemy action. Fortunately, this powerful IJN force did not press home its advantage, and the amphibious transports got most of their heavy equipment ashore before departing on 9 August.

Mackinac's position was also assessed as too dangerous following the Savo Island disaster, and VP-23's det flew off to Noumea that same day as the tender slipped away to safety. Scouting and patrol work in the campaign was henceforth performed by *Curtiss'* PBYs.

Despite the Battle of Savo Island placing a grievous strain on those ashore, this proved to be only a temporary setback, as the Marines, shorn of offshore support, nevertheless proved themselves to be formidable antagonists. What they took, they held, including the all-important airstrip at Lunga Point, which was christened Henderson Field in honour of Marine Corps SBD pilot Maj Lofton Henderson, who had been killed leading VMSB-241 into action during the Battle of Midway.

On 12 August, a PBY became the first aircraft ever to land on Henderson Field when Admiral McCain's PBY-5A BuNo 05045, flown by Lt W S Sampson, delivered urgent supplies and departed the next morning with two wounded Marines. The audacity in making such a flight in the face of frequent enemy air attacks showed the Marines that they had not been abandoned. US Navy construction teams were subsequently lifted in, and together with Marine engineers, Henderson Field was made marginally ready.

Admiral John S McCain's PBY-5A BuNo 05045 is seen at Henderson Field on 12 August 1942 shortly after becoming the first aircraft ever to land on the Guadalcanal airstrip

Only a week later (on 20 August), 12 Marine Corps SBD Dauntlesses from VMSB-223 took off from the escort carrier USS *Long Island* and flew into Henderson. The next day, 19 F4F Wildcats from VMF-223 departed the vessel and also headed for Henderson Field. The base was now operational, and Japanese aircraft sent to bomb Guadalcanal became aware of this fact on 22 August, when Wildcats gave them a mauling.

BATTLE OF THE EASTERN SOLOMONS

FRUPAC alerted CINCPAC that the IJN's carrier force was going to make a serious attempt to retake Guadalcanal in late August, so Nimitz made sure that he had his carriers in place to defend the island against any such attack. Once again, he would rely on the searching PBYs to actually find and flush out the quarry for the carrier- and land-based aircraft that would then hunt the Japanese vessels down.

The third of the four big carrier-versus-carrier battles that rocked the Pacific in 1942, the Battle of the Eastern Solomons started off with a near 'friendly fire' incident on 24 August. A small number of PBYs from VP-11 and VP-23 were operating from USS *Mackinac* and USS *Ballard* at Ndeni, in the Santa Cruz Islands, as this forward position allowed the Catalinas to extend their sector searches well to the north over waters through which, according to COMINT, the enemy thrust would come.

While the PBYs continued their round-the-clock searches, Admiral Fletcher in *Saratoga*, supported by *Enterprise* and *Wasp*, waited anxiously for the VP units to find targets for his carrier strike groups. The carriers, of course, mounted their own search using their SBD scouting squadrons, although the PBYs had a much greater reach. And it was two Dauntlesses from *Wasp* that spotted the tenders at their remote anchorage during one such search patrol. Reporting their find, they readied themselves for an attack, but fortunately their carrier called them off.

In the fast moving air-sea battles that were now being fought in the Pacific, rapid, reliable communications, and a sharp look out, were critical to victory, and survival. *Mackinac* and *Ballard* were in fact very exposed, not just to *Wasp*'s aircraft but potentially to IJN carrier fighters and dive-bombers as well. Still, the exposure was thought warranted because of the immense reconnaissance contribution the PBYs could, and did, make to the tactical picture as the enemy approached.

The Santa Cruz Islands lay southeast of the Solomons, and on 25 August VP-23 worked out six patrol areas covering the enemy's anticipated approach. These narrow, contiguous sectors reached out 650 miles, with the left-most sector paralleling the Solomons chain, 306 to 313 degrees from *Mackinac* at Ndeni. This sector was flown by '23-P-1' (radio call sign '1V37', or 'One Victor Three Seven'), with Ens Theodore S Thueson at the controls. To the right, in the next seven-degree sector (313 to 320 degrees), was '23-P-3' ('3V37'), flown by Lt Joseph M Kellum, then '23-P-5' ('5V37'), with Ens Gale C Burkey at the controls, covering 320 to 327 degrees. Ens James A Spraggins in '23-P-7' ('7V37') patrolled sector

The 1760-ton USS *Mackinac* was a new *Barnegat*-class tender commissioned into the US Navy in early 1942 and sent to serve with the Pacific Fleet. Active alongside other tenders in the South Pacific for much of 1942-43, the vessel mounted two 5-in turrets forward. *Mackinac* was one of three small seaplane tenders present in Tokyo Bay during the Japanese surrender ceremony held aboard the battleship USS *Missouri* on 2 September 1945

Working dangerously far forward of the main Allied force in the Solomons, a PBY-5 from VP-23 refuels 'over the stern' of *Mackinac*, anchored off Ndeni, in the Santa Cruz Islands, in October 1942. PBYs made a stunningly important contribution to the winning of the Battle of Santa Cruz (*Dave's Warbirds*)

327-334 degrees, whilst in the right-most areas were '23-P-8' ('8V37'), flown by Lt(jg) Robert E Slater, and, flying the 341-348 degrees sector, Lt Leo B Riester in '23-P-9' ('9V37').

The VP-11 PBYs were also involved in this search operation too, covering other areas.

All Catalinas committed to the search were sent off before dawn on the 25th, and they began making contact with Japanese forces at 0937 hrs. Radiomen aboard *Enterprise* received the following message from Ens Burkey's '5V37' – 'One carrier, two cruisers, four destroyers, 4-40S, 161-15E, course 180'. The PBY had spotted the light carrier *Ryujo*, but the overall tactical picture was far from clear, and the PBY's identification imprecise. The Americans knew, however, if heavy fleet units had been found then the big carriers could not be far away.

Then, at 1005 hrs, Ens Thueson's '1V37' reported being attacked by three enemy fighters. Admiral Fletcher realised that these aircraft could in fact be shore-based Zero-sens from Bougainville, and not carrier-based fighters. Adding further to the confusion, the call sign for the first signal from Burkey had been missed by *Enterprise*'s radiomen, and it was thus thought that both reports had come from Thueson's PBY. The significance of Burkey's first report, therefore, went unrecognised.

Within minutes came a third report from Lt Riester's crew in '23-P-9' ('9V37'), who stated that 'two heavy cruisers and two destroyers' had been located in a position to the northeast of the first sightings. What the PBY crew had actually discovered was Vice Admiral Nobutake Kondo's battleships and the seaplane carrier *Chitose*, which immediately launched at least three F1M 'Petes' to intercept the Catalina. The biplane scouts worked over Riester's PBY and killed the second pilot, Ens Robert Wilcox, sat in the right hand seat. Whilst this was going on, the radioman promptly keyed out a follow up message – 'Attacked by aircraft, fighting type Zeros'. Once again this was a technically imprecise report, and thus misleading for those listening out for the transmission.

Upon receiving this report Admiral Fletcher naturally assumed that Riester had encountered the carrier force, as his radioman had reported being attacked by Zero-sens, which were naval fighters – no land-based A6Ms could be this far to the east. This was a false conclusion, of course, as *Chitose*, with its handful of 'Pete' floatplanes, was by no means an aircraft carrier! Lt(jg) Slater in the neighbouring sector also fought off F1Ms, and reported being attacked by 'unidentified' fighters.

It was Ens Burkey's PBY that finally encountered Vice Admiral Chuichi Nagumo's big fleet carriers, and *Saratoga* copied '5V37's' second report of the morning at 1110 hrs – 'One carrier, two cruisers, four destroyers, 4-40S, 161-20E, course 180'. The difference in the positions between this sighting and Burkey's first at 0937 hrs when he saw *Ryujo* indicates that the latter vessel had been seen after it broke away from

Nagumo's main force so as to cover the invasion convoy. The vessel sighted in this new report, made more than an hour later, was either *Shokaku* or *Zuikaku*, which were the two fleet carriers committed to the retaking of Guadalacanal. With one of the primary targets now located, the battle entered a new phase.

The crews flying the PBYs shadowing the Japanese warships now found themselves in a hazardous position as fighters from both sides went in search of targets to attack. At 1150 hrs *Saratoga's* Fighter Direction Officer (FDO) located a 'bogie' at 'two six zero angels twelve' (unidentified aircraft bearing 260 degrees at an altitude of 12,000 ft) on his radar and vectored out part of his CAP that was on station overhead the carrier to intercept. Using the call sign 'Scarlet 7', Lt Dave Richardson and his wingman in their F4Fs peered through the gaps in heavy cloud as they strived not to miss the radar contact.

Two minutes later, and 30 miles from the ship, the CAP voice circuit crackled to life. 'On our port bow', Richardson's wingman reported. 'Up or down?' replied the lead Wildcat pilot, who then saw the target as well – 'Tally ho, one Kawanishi'. They had correctly identified the IJN's PBY flying-boat equivalent, the four-engined Kawanishi H8K 'Emily' flying-boat. This particular example was from the Yokohoma Air Group, based in the Solomon's Shortland Islands chain to the northwest of Guadalcanal. Its crew was performing exactly the same mission as that given to VP-23's PBYs, and the flying-boat was downed with the same clinical precision by the Wildcat pilots as had been the fate of numerous Catalinas intercepted by Zero-sens in the past nine months.

The opportunity of a fratricidal incident taking place when land-based friendly aircraft flew anywhere near a carrier task force was very high, as fighter pilots manning the CAP – be they American or Japanese – were always excited when an unidentified contact was announced by the ship-based FDO. Thus, when 'Red Base' (*Enterprise's* FDO) radioed the Wildcat pilots to tell them that he had a low altitude 'bogie' showing up on his radar screen, bearing 340 degrees and closing, he vectored out Lt(jg) 'Scoop' Vorse, call sign 'Red 5', in his F4F to intercept the contact. The Wildcat pilot was sent on his way with the admonition to get right on him, as from the FDO's viewpoint, the 'bogie' could well have been a deadly Japanese torpedo-bomber.

Fortunately for Lt Joseph Kellum and his crew in '23-P-3', Vorse's trained eye told him that the contact he was about to gun down was, in fact, a PBY. He eyeballed the flying-boat carefully, nonetheless, as the F4F pilot was well aware that some Catalinas had been captured in the Dutch East Indies, and the Japanese may be 'pulling a fast one'. However, he soon pronounced the headstrong intruder 'clean', and Kellum duly flew right over the formation of ships at great risk, contacted *Enterprise* by Aldis lamp, and reported a small

The Kawanishi H8K 'Emily' flying-boat was a more modern contemporary of the PBY, performing the same kind of hazardous long-range reconnaissance patrolling for the IJN that was the Catalina's lot in the Pacific War. The H8K was a fast, well-armed aircraft, but it was no match for US Navy fighters or, in this particular case, a VB-115 PB4Y-1

enemy carrier bearing 320 degrees at a distance 195 miles. The flagship acknowledged his report, at which point Kellum turned for *Mackinac*.

The subsequent Battle of the Eastern Solomons, fought on 25-26 August, again saw US carriers triumph over their Japanese rivals, as SBDs sank *Ryujo* and badly damaged *Shokaku*. This large-scale action thus defeated the enemy's efforts to throw the Marines Corps off Guadalcanal.

Although the main carrier clash was all over in less than 48 hours, both sides continued to trade blows on a smaller, but no less committed, scale in the Solomons over subsequent weeks. And with war being a dynamic, minute-by-minute activity, confusion frequently reigns, and inevitably mistakes occur. These were precisely the circumstances that befell a PBY crew on the night of 5 September.

The fast transports USS *Little* and USS *Gregory* had arrived with crucially needed reinforcements and supplies early that day, and they were anchored off Lunga Point until night fall, when they were scheduled to offload their cargo. Fatefully, that same night the Japanese destroyers *Yudachi, Murakumo* and *Hatsuyuki* were making the now frequent 'Tokyo Express' run with troops and supplies for the defenders of Guadalcanal – some 6000 soldiers were landed in this way following the US invasion. A PBY on night patrol, searching for IJN vessels performing this hazardous mission, spotted what it thought were enemy ships and dropped flares to illuminate them so that Marine gunners ashore might retaliate. The flare drop worked perfectly, but the ships that the crew had seen were *Little* and *Gregory*. With the American vessels thus illuminated, the destroyer *Yudachi* promptly opened fire with its five-inch main battery and sank both ships, causing many casualties.

TORPEDO-BOMBER

With things growing increasingly desperate for the embattled Americans on Guadalcanal, and replacement aircraft being in particularly short supply, Catalinas occasionally found themselves being asked to perform missions to which they were not always suited. One such example occurred on 14 October when the PBY-5A assigned to the new commanding officer for all Allied aircraft in the Solomons, Marine General Roy S Geiger (an experienced Naval Aviator), was used to ferry up two torpedoes for US Navy TBF Avenger unit VT-8, which was shore-based at Henderson strip at the time.

Upon the PBY-5A's arrival on the island, its crew was told that a Japanese supply convoy was approaching and that all the torpedo-bombers were unserviceable. The Catalina's pilot, Maj Jack Cram, proposed to deliver the torpedoes himself if General Geiger approved his plan – which he did.

Although the PBY had indeed been built to drop torpedoes, the required racks for mounting these weapons were not at hand, so a release method for them had to be jury rigged. Following several hours of frantic work on the Catalina, the aircraft finally took off in the late afternoon and soon found the enemy transports, with their destroyer escorts, just a few miles east of the Marine Corps beachhead off Tassafaronga. Cram attacked in a shallow dive from 6000 ft, skipping over a destroyer and then aiming his torpedoes at two transports. Despite being opposed by a ferocious barrage of flak, the PBY-5A escaped relatively unscathed. The

General Roy Geiger's PBY-5A, seen here at Henderson Field, was pressed into service as a torpedo-bomber on 14 October 1942 (*Dave's Warbirds*)

same could not be said for one of the transports, however, which erupted with a blinding flash.

Maj Cram then flew back to Henderson with a few souvenir bullet holes in the general's personal aeroplane. Geiger did not hold the latter against him, however, instead awarding Cram the Navy Cross!

This mission was certainly a one-off for the PBY force in the Solomons, with long-ranging patrols monitoring the enemy's movements usually being the first priority for VP units. The Pacific Fleet's battleships, cruisers and destroyers were now well and truly engaged with their Japanese counterparts in a lengthy 'slugfest' for control of the Solomon Islands. The Battle of the Eastern Solomons had resulted in victory, but the *Saratoga* had subsequently been damaged by a Japanese submarine on 31 August and the *Wasp* sunk in yet another torpedo attack on 15 September. Reduced in strength to just a solitary carrier (*Hornet*) and surface ships, the Pacific Fleet now relied more than ever on Japanese fleet movements being accurately monitored over the horizon by the PBYs.

And patrolling Catalinas posed a threat to smaller enemy ships if discovered by the aircraft, as the flying-boat's two 500-lb demolition bombs could inflict serious damage to thin-skinned destroyers, barges, transports and coasters.

Aside from looking for Japanese ships, the patrolling PBY crews also played their part as the Allies fought to wrest air superiority from the enemy over ever-increasing chunks of the Pacific theatre. Regularly flying into harm's way in the Solomons during September and October, VP units paid a high price during this period of sustained operations. '11-P-5' went down on 6 September after tangling with an aggressively flown Kawanishi H6K 'Mavis', and '11-P-10' was lost five days later after being set upon by several F1Ms – its crew was captured. On 14 September carrier Zero-sens flamed Lt Baxter Moore's '23-P-4' (BuNo 04433), while Lt(jg) Melvin K Butler and crew, in '91-P-7' (BuNo 04509), failed to return from a patrol later that same day. VP-91 lost '91-P-2' and '91-P-11' 48 hours later.

The Kawanishi H6K 'Mavis' also roamed the Pacific scouting out the Pacific Fleet throughout the war, and one even shot down a PBY in the Solomons in September 1942. This particular example was despatched by carrier-borne F6F Hellcats (*US Navy*)

Seaplane tender *McFarland* also fell victim to enemy action when, on 16 October, the vessel was hit by a bomb whilst transporting ammunition and aviation fuel, and towing a barge load of bombs, to Guadalcanal. The vessel limped across the 'Slot' to Tulagi and made good its escape, but it had been a close run thing.

In a more positive development, a patrolling VP-11 PBY, flown by Lt F J Hill, spotted the Japanese submarine I-172 surfaced off Guadalcanal on 29 October and quickly sank the vessel.

Just prior to this rash of PBY losses, CINCPAC had made PatWing 1 a mobile command. Nimitz subsequently sent the wing CO, along with VP-72 and VP-91, to Noumea to personally direct VP operations in mid-September. VP-72 relieved VP-71 once in-theatre, and VP-24 deployed to relieve VP-23 on 1 October. COMPATWING 1 moved forward to Espiritu Santo and the tender *Curtiss* on 1 December.

THE BATTLE OF SANTA CRUZ

The fourth, and last, of the big carrier battles of 1942, fought off the islands of Santa Cruz between 25 and 27 October, was as complex and intense an action as any of the previous three clashes. FRUPAC had again alerted Nimitz at Pearl Harbor of an impending attempt by the IJN to seize Guadalcanal by drawing the Pacific Fleet into a decisive action, and CINCPAC had immediately placed Vice Admiral Halsey's carrier force in the South Pacific on alert. This time six aircraft carriers would be involved – four Japanese and two American. To date in 1942, both navies had lost nine carriers in action between them, and this battle would see another one sent to the bottom and three others badly damaged.

Admiral Aubrey Fitch's Air Force South Pacific (AirSoPac) handled the long-range patrol work in the lead up to the battle, with ten PBYs and six USAAF B-17s covering the northern semi-circle from 'Button' (Espiritu Santo) out some 650 to 800 miles on a daily basis. Commander PatWing 1 based his PBYs primarily with *Curtiss* at Espiritu Santo, while the small tender USS *Ballard*, anchored at Vanikoro, in the Santa Cruz Islands, added aircraft conducting longer-ranged scouting. Once again, the latter vessel was very exposed to enemy action in this forward position, but it proved vital in supporting the operations of mostly VP-91 PBY-5s – in practice, VP crews and aeroplanes were now being frequently pooled in order to get the job done.

A USAAF B-17 from Henderson Field found the enemy's 'advance force' at 0930 hrs on 25 October, and ten minutes later *Ballard's* '91-P-14', flown by Lt(jg) Warren B Matthew and crew, spotted the 'vanguard force' and sent off their reports. Neither force included the carriers, but nevertheless they were nearby. Two very aggressive 'Pete' floatplanes from the battleship *Kirishima* chased Matthew away from the warships, holing the PBY and damaging its port engine. The aircraft ducked into a cloud and succeeded in shadowing the force for some time, but neither *Curtiss* or *Enterprise* picked up its contact reports!

It was '24-P-7', flown by Lt(jg) Robert T Lampshire and crew, covering the 338-344 degrees sector from *Ballard*, that hit the jackpot. It found Nagumo's *Kido Butai* and transmitted the first of several reports, identifying carriers, battleships and cruisers at a point more than 300 miles north of *Ballard* and twice that distance from *Curtiss* at Espiritu Santo. The report also noted that the crew had seen a carrier (the light carrier *Zuiho*) launching fighters. Minutes later, '24-P-7's' crew radioed that they could see two more large carriers – *Shokaku* and *Zuikaku*.

Admiral Thomas Kinkaid, CTF 61 in *Enterprise*, soon had Lampshire's reports, rebroadcast by *Ballard*, and on the chart the plot showed the enemy carriers still 375 miles north of his vessels. Although they were well out of striking range, Kincaid now knew the Japanese were present in force, and precisely where. Once again, COMINT had provided the critically important advanced warning, with the seasoned PBY crews knowing when and where to look, which in turn allowed them to make contact while the enemy was still some distance away.

Meanwhile, on Guadalcanal, the Japanese 17th Army launched an offensive to recapture Henderson Field, this new push being timed to coincide with the impending arrival of the powerful carrier force. The gritty Marines stood their ground, both in the jungle and in the air,

expending vast quantities of ammunition. There ability to hold the line on the island made the difference, as the Japanese desperately wanted to operate their own aircraft from Henderson Field so as to strike at the numerous American warships in the waters around Guadalcanal.

During the night of 25-26 October, five radar-equipped PBYs prowled northeast of the island in search of the Japanese task force. Lt(jg) George S Clute of VP-11, flying '51-P-8', spotted the enemy formation just minutes after midnight about 300 miles northwest of the US fleet and attacked with his torpedo. The latter narrowly missed the destroyer *Isokaze* in the vanguard force.

The *Kido Butai* was only 20 miles away to the north, and Admiral Nagumo wondered whether, in the bright moonlight, his carriers had been sighted. His question was answered at 0250 hrs by '91-P-3', flown by Lt Glen Hoffman and crew, whose glide-bombing attack just missed *Zuikaku* with a pair of 500-lb bombs. This singular attack, which had come so very close to hitting the carrier with its morning strike aeroplanes already fuelled and armed, caused Admiral Nagumo to feel he was perhaps sailing into a trap set by the Americans. With the disaster at Midway still fresh in his mind, he personally ordered the formation to countermarch, and the aeroplanes to be defuelled and disarmed.

Zuikaku subsequently launched its morning strike at 0900 hrs on the 26th, and this whole evolution was observed by two of *Ballard*'s PBYs. The VP-24 Catalina, piloted by Lt(jg) Enos L Jones, radioed a contact report, which was followed shortly afterwards by Lt(jg) George F Poulos' sighting in '11-P-8'. The latter saw one carrier – probably *Zuikaku* – very clearly, and his radioman immediately began transmitting. However, it was not until 0925 hrs that *Curtiss* acknowledged his signal. Chased by several aggressive enemy fighters, Poulos pressed for more informartion, and then broke away into a cloud and withdrew.

Besides '11-P-8', several other PBYs retransmitted sighting reports until satisfied that *Curtiss* had received them. Admiral Kinkaid did not receive this intelligence until mid-afternoon – communications handling was still proving to be a constant challenge in this vast theatre.

On the return leg of their long patrol, Lt(jg) Norm Haber and crew, in '24-P-6', ran afoul of seven Zero-sens from the light carrier *Junyo*. Returning after their strike on the Pacific Fleet, and doubtless low on fuel and ammunition, the fighters made only two half-hearted passes at the flying-boat and then continued on their way. They nevertheless claimed a 'Consolidated' – the Japanese pilots' jargon for a PBY – shot down. The aircraft had indeed taken some hits, but its gunners had given as good as they got and the Catalina flew on.

Having survived this attack, the crew then almost fell victim to aircraft from their own side. The sky was full of carrier fighters, dive- and torpedo-bombers desperately trying to find somewhere to land, as the

As a large tender, USS *Curtiss* was equipped with heavy lift cranes that could easily hoist a PBY on board. This allowed the vessel to undertake a wide range of maintenance tasks for deployed seaplane squadrons operating in the South Pacific

The eyes of the fleet – a PBY crewman on watch in the waist blister. His eyes were a key tool in the VP squadrons' reconnaissance mission. The crewman was able to talk directly to the pilot forward via a throat microphone. The entire crew relied on the skill and watchfulness of the observers in the blisters (*US Navy*)

Hornet had been mortally damaged. And although *Enterprise* was withdrawing southward with a jammed flightdeck elevator, the carrier was doing its best to recover as many aeroplanes from both 'flattops' as it could. By midday, only a dozen TBFs on anti-submarine patrols remained overhead the vessel.

Shortly after 1200 hrs, *Enterprise's* radar picked up a 'bogey', and the crew worried about a possible follow-up attack by the IJN. With its F4Fs having landed, only the TBFs now stood between the Pacific Fleet's sole remaining carrier in-theatre and a potential aerial assault. At 1205 hrs, *Enterprise's* FDO, Lt Jack Griffen, used the search frequency to entreat 'any SBD with fuel to investigate bogey', but there were no takers. Five minutes later he called, 'Any "Reaper" fish answer', and Griffen instructed 'any' TBF to check out the 'bogey' bearing 030 degrees, distance 25 miles. Six Avengers responded, and they went after the contact that was now swinging around to the east. The TBF-1 was ill-suited to the CAP mission now thrust upon it, as it boasted only a single 0.30-cal 'peashooter' firing forward.

A few minutes later, 'Shorty' Griffen issued a recall order when the 'bogey' turned out to be a PBY. As in August, *Enterprise* had entertained considerable suspicion that the Japanese might be flying a rogue Catalina. However, it was none other than Norm Haber's battered PBY that had fought seven Zero-sens to a standstill. He initially sighted the doomed destroyer USS *Porter* in its final death throes, then TF-16 itself. Four hours later Haber set down at Espiritu Santo without rudder or elevator control. '24-P-6' sported some 144 bullet holes (78 aft of the rear blisters to the tail). Haber and his crew had survived a remarkable mission, their courage and skill exemplifying the AirSoPac search crews' efforts in 1942.

Although *Hornet* had been sunk and *Enterprise* left badly damaged, the Battle of Santa Cruz had seen Japanese attempts to force the Marines from Guadalcanal thwarted a fourth time. The PBYs had played their role to near perfection in the lead up to the carrier clash, and they continued to take the fight to the enemy after the 'flattops' had disengaged.

On the evening of 26 October three torpedo-carrying PBYs departed Espiritu Santo to hunt carriers. At around midnight, Lt(jg) Donald Jackson and crew in '51-P-6' found *Junyo*, and their torpedo missed by only a small margin. An hour later, '91-P-3', manned by Lt Melvin K Atwell and crew, dropped two 500-lb bombs on a 'cruiser', the weapons killing or wounding nearly 50 of the ship's crew, which turned out to be a destroyer screening the carrier *Zuikaku*. By now the IJN was withdrawing the remnants of its fleet further west.

The PBY force's final contribution to the Battle of Santa Cruz came on 28 October when VP-23's Lt(jg) William T O'Dowd and his crew spotted and recovered VS-8's commanding officer, Lt Cdr Gus Widhelm, and his radioman George Stokely, whose SBD had been shot down by Zero-sens 48 hours earlier. Such experienced aircrew were far from expendable.

The PBY force in-theatre had also suffered its fair share of casualties too, and between May and December 1942 six different squadrons in the South Pacific had lost 22 PBYs between them, with seven of these falling to Japanese aircraft.

MORE FIGHTING IN THE ALEUTIANS

Despite their base appearing to be in the grips of a blizzard, long-suffering sailors from VP-42 get their mount ready for an impending patrol by sweeping away snow and chipping off ice somewhere in the Aleutians in 1942

As mentioned in the previous chapter, Japanese forces had invaded the Aleutian islands in June 1942, and PatWing 4's PBYs fought both the enemy and the weather throughout the second half of the year. Flying from Kodiak, aircrew continually battled the cold, with ice and freezing conditions hindering all machinery, and limiting operations on the water and in the air. When not frozen, land-based operations encountered mud literally everywhere. Visibility was usually very limited too, always variable and often simply reduced to zero, with wind direction severe and frequently changing. To make matters worse, numerous mountains on the many islands that made up the Aleutians posed a serious navigational hazard to the crews as they attempted to navigate their way through the nearly constant low clouds and fog.

The weather played no favourites, however, and the enemy suffered as well. Still, even when PatWing 4 moved its operations forward to Kodiak, the wing's PBYs based in the Aleutians were still 1000 miles further west.

The amphibious capacity of the PBY-5A proved very useful in this theatre, and PatWing 4's VP-41 and VP-42 had been among the first squadrons to take delivery of this variant in the spring of 1942. VP-43 and VP-61 would subsequently follow both units north with still more amphibious Catalinas.

After excellent work during the 'Kiska Blitz', and the recovery of the Zero-sen on Akutan Island (also detailed in the previous chapter), VP-41 was ordered to Seattle and stood down on 1 August 1942. It was to become the first PBY unit to convert to a dedicated land-based type in the form of the Lockheed PV-1 Ventura, the unit being redesignated as VB-136 as part of the type change. Likewise, in October, most of VP-51 was sent to San Diego to transition to Consolidated PB4Y-1 Liberators as VB-101.

Aside from enduring some of the worst weather imaginable for soldiering, the Japanese invaders on the occupied islands were also harassed during regular nuisance raids performed by the PBYs. Many re-supply missions did manage to make it through to bring in food, ammunition and equipment for the occupying force, the vessels making the most of the frequently poor weather to escape the attentions of the far-reaching PBY scouts.

These PBY-5s from VP-61 were blown off their beaching trolleys at Dutch Harbor during a 'Williwaw' – wind storms that blighted the Aleutians – on 21 November 1942. Note the radar antenna beneath the wing of the aircraft in the foreground. VP-61 was the sole operator of the 'Dash 5' in the Aleutians at the time (*Roger Ferguson*)

VP-61's 'Boat 25' was badly damaged during the 21 November 1942 'Williwaw' (*Roger Ferguson*)

Nevertheless, the presence of the Catalinas, or the mere threat of them, kept the enemy from attempting more substantial efforts to keep the troops re-supplied.

In August the seaplane tender USS *Casco* moved forward to Nazan Bay, off Atka, and VP-61 sent two PBYs to operate with the vessel. However, on the 30th of that same month an IJN submarine torpedoed the warship and its crew had to carry out an emergency beaching in order for repairs to be effected.

Other PBYs from VP-42 and VP-43 were assigned to operate from USS *Teal* at Adak, and it was from here that patrolling aircraft spotted a submarine on the surface on several separate occasions on 31 August. Their quarry was RO-61, which had all but sunk *Casco* the previous day. The vessel hastily submerged following each sighting, although it was severely damaged by depth charges dropped by the PBY-5As of Lt S E Colman and Lt Carl H Amme. The latter, from VP-42, guided in the destroyer USS *Reid* to finish off the submarine, which 'battle surfaced' and attempted to fight off its enemies. The destroyer made short work of RO-61, which capsized and sank.

Despite this success, the PBY force continued to fall foul of the weather conditions. In July, VP-43's Lt Green had flown into a mountain on Atka, and on 23 August Lt Raither and his crew failed to return from a patrol flight. In November, an Aleutian 'Williwaw' flipped 'Boat 25' onto its back in Dutch Harbor, and as the year drew to a close the weather only got worse.

Keen to keep the Japanese from expanding their presence in the Aleutians, the Army decided that it needed to go on the offensive and strike out further west through the occupation of Amchitka. Maj B B Talley led a reconnaissance team to the island in December, where they found ample evidence that the Japanese had been there – in fact they had been planning to occupy Amchitka as well. Talley and his team quickly determined that an airfield could be built here to help with its reinforcement. He quickly determined to head back to Kodiak to deliver his report in person, with the marathon Unmak to Kodiak leg of his trip being made in a war-weary US Navy PBY – flown by Ens Thomas Ewing – that was scheduled for an overhaul.

Ens Thomas Ewing's PatWing 4 PBY-5 sinks in the Gulf of Alaska in December 1942. A commissioned ex-NAP enlisted pilot, Ewing had been Lt Bergstrom's second pilot during numerous 'Kiska Blitz' missions, and was a seasoned flier (*Robert Bergstrom*)

In a harrowing experience for all involved, the PBY lost an engine before reaching its destination and went down in the Gulf of Alaska. Talley was convinced that he and the crew survived only because of former enlisted pilot Ewing's skill at the controls. A destroyer quickly rescued them from the freezing water, and Talley made his report.

Sixty days later USAAF fighters were flying from a new strip on Amchitka.

Amchitka Island, in the Aleutians. This formidable location had an airstrip built on it in early 1943

ORGANISING FOR VICTORY

Away from the fighting in the Solomons and the Aleutians, CINCPAC Admiral Nimitz established a new administrative command on 1 September 1942 – Commander US Naval Air Forces, Pacific Fleet, which was shortened to COMNAVAIRPAC for daily use. This position was initially filled by Rear Admiral Aubury Fitch in Pearl Harbor. He had authority over the existing Commander Carriers, Pacific Fleet, and Commander Patrol Wings, Pacific Fleet, and both positions were subsequently abolished. These changes at last meant that all US Navy and Marine Corps aviation activities in the Pacific came under a common head, and management of the flow of resources to all carrier-, shore-, and tender-based air units would now be smoother as a result.

Most importantly, the establishment of COMNAVAIRPAC would ensure both adequate control and the streamlining of pilot and aircrew advanced combat training, both on the west coast and in Hawaii, as new and reformed squadrons and replacement Naval Aviators moved forward into the frontline.

Patrol wings both multiplied and adjusted following this change. PatWing 1 would remain the Pacific Fleet's most mobile VP organisation, with its units operating from a long list of exotic locations up to VJ-Day. PatWing 2, on the other hand, would remain in Hawaii throughout the war, acting as a 'central clearing house' for VP squadrons and crews. PatWing 4 operated its PBYs from Kodiak during its service in the North Pacific.

Back on the west coast of the USA, Alameda-based PatWing 8 expanded in October 1942 to oversee the operations of both PatWing 14 in San Diego and Fleet Air Wing (FAW) 6 in Seattle (the latter soon moving to newly-built NAS Whidbey Island) the following month. These three wings managed all VP and PBY activity on the west coast through to war's end.

The constantly evolving nature of non-carrier based naval aviation led to the redesignation on 1 November of all Patrol Wings as Fleet Air Wings (FAWs). These administrative changes were the last to affect the PBY units in World War 2, although in detail things continued to evolve until VJ-Day.

Rear Admiral Aubrey Fitch was made the very first COMNAVAIRPAC by CINCPAC Admiral Nimitz on 1 September 1942. This title gave him control over all US Navy aircraft, both land- and sea-based, in the Pacific theatre

COLOUR PLATES

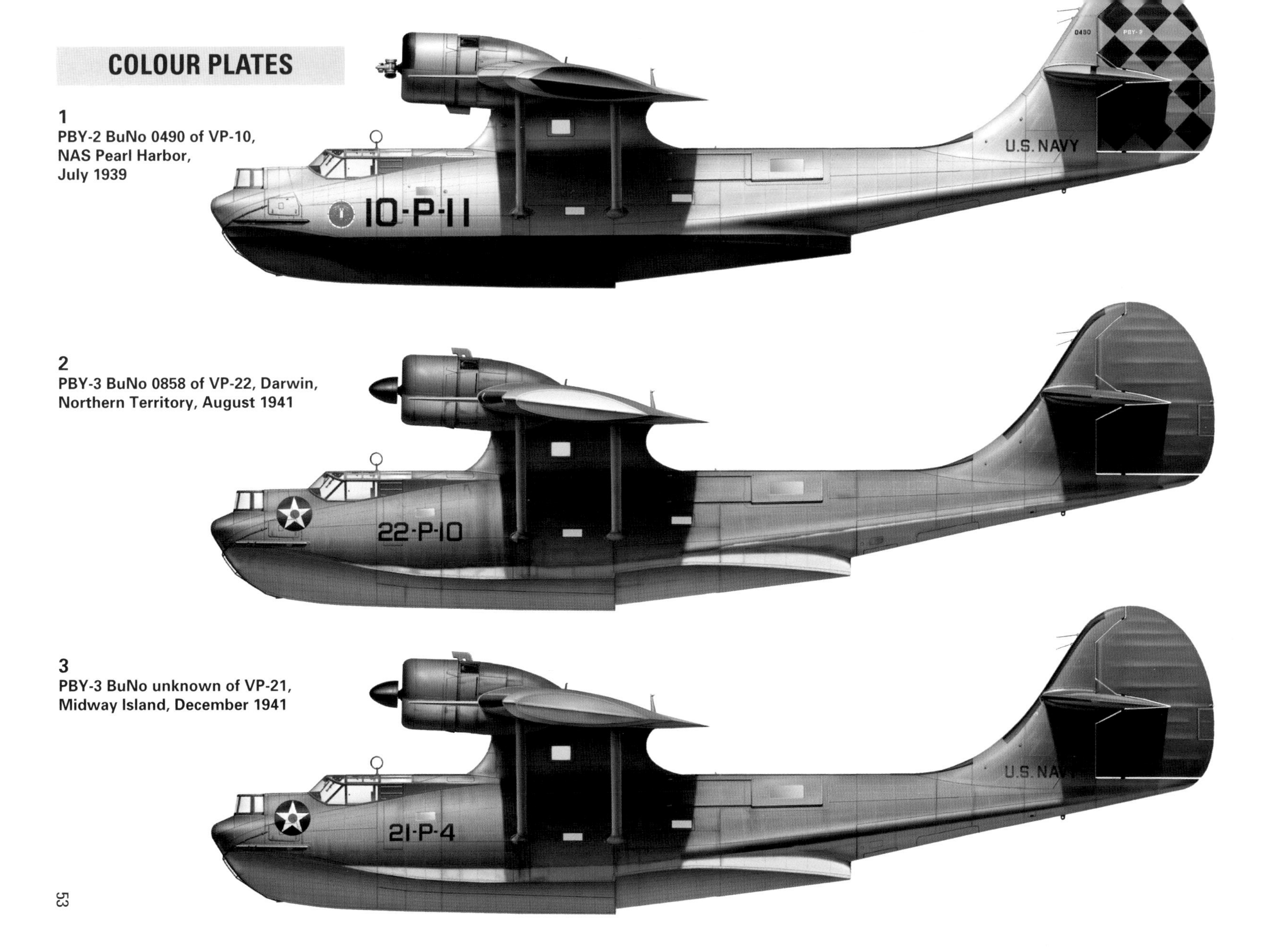

1
PBY-2 BuNo 0490 of VP-10,
NAS Pearl Harbor,
July 1939

2
PBY-3 BuNo 0858 of VP-22, Darwin,
Northern Territory, August 1941

3
PBY-3 BuNo unknown of VP-21,
Midway Island, December 1941

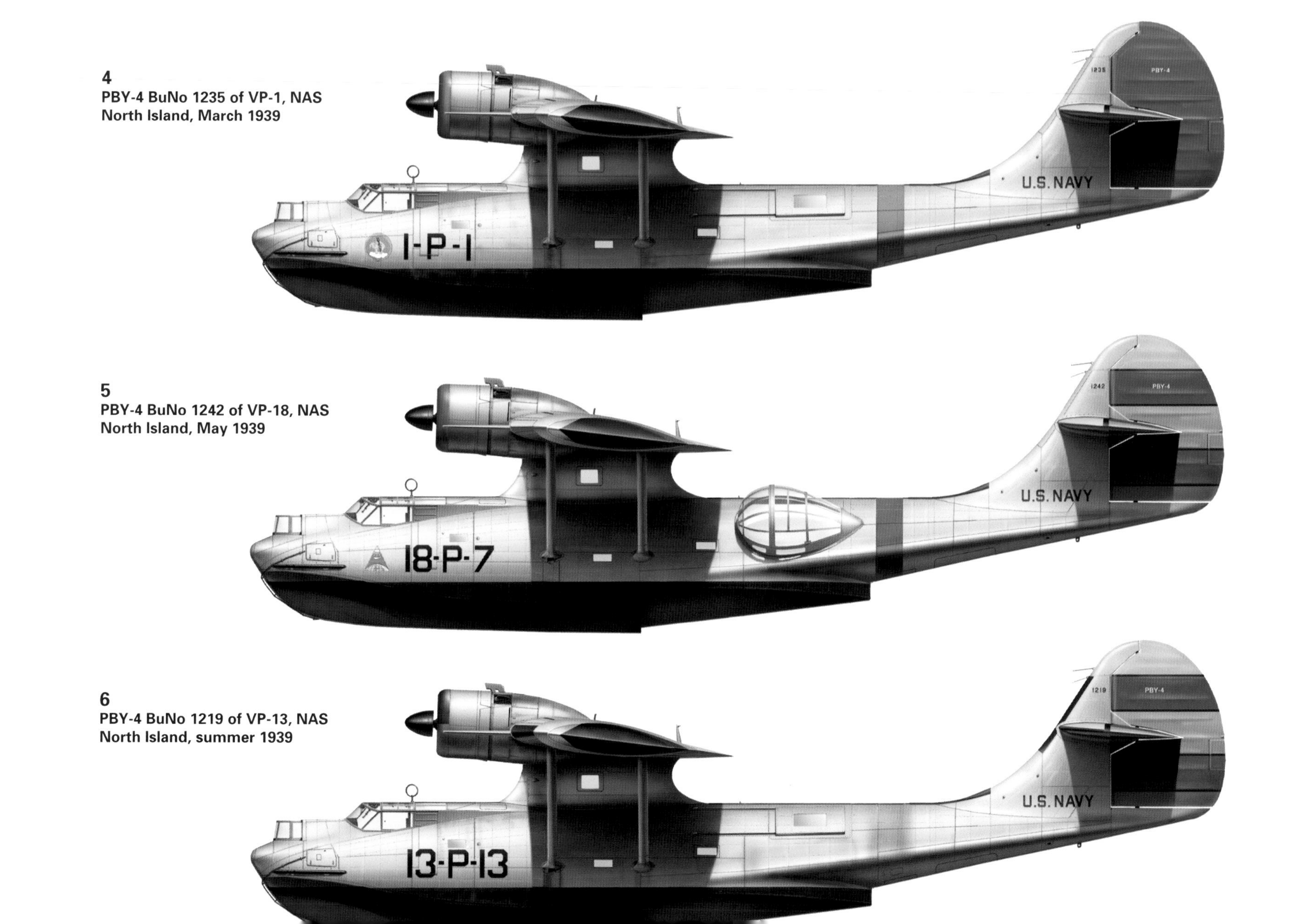

4
PBY-4 BuNo 1235 of VP-1, NAS North Island, March 1939

5
PBY-4 BuNo 1242 of VP-18, NAS North Island, May 1939

6
PBY-4 BuNo 1219 of VP-13, NAS North Island, summer 1939

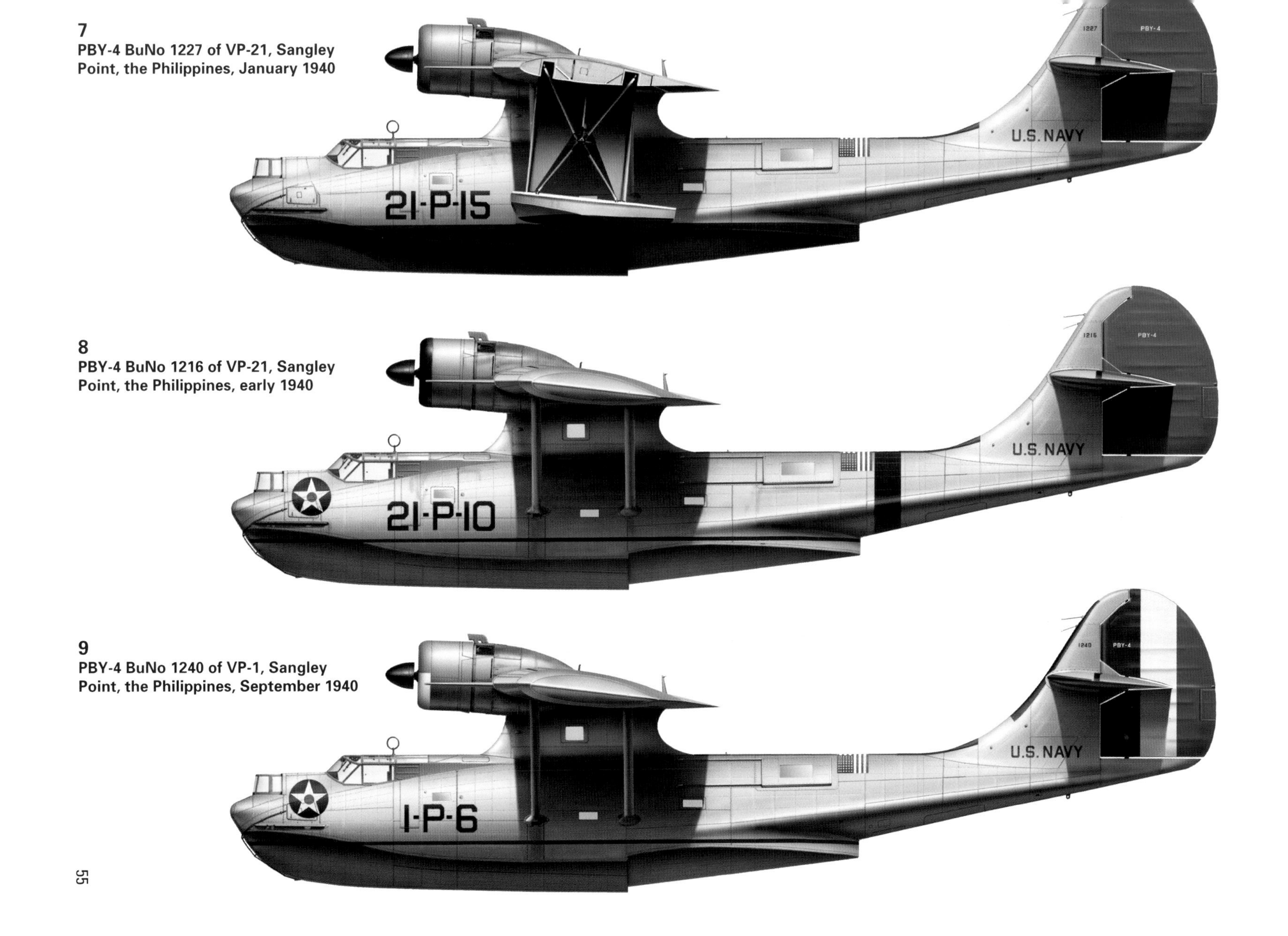

7
PBY-4 BuNo 1227 of VP-21, Sangley Point, the Philippines, January 1940

8
PBY-4 BuNo 1216 of VP-21, Sangley Point, the Philippines, early 1940

9
PBY-4 BuNo 1240 of VP-1, Sangley Point, the Philippines, September 1940

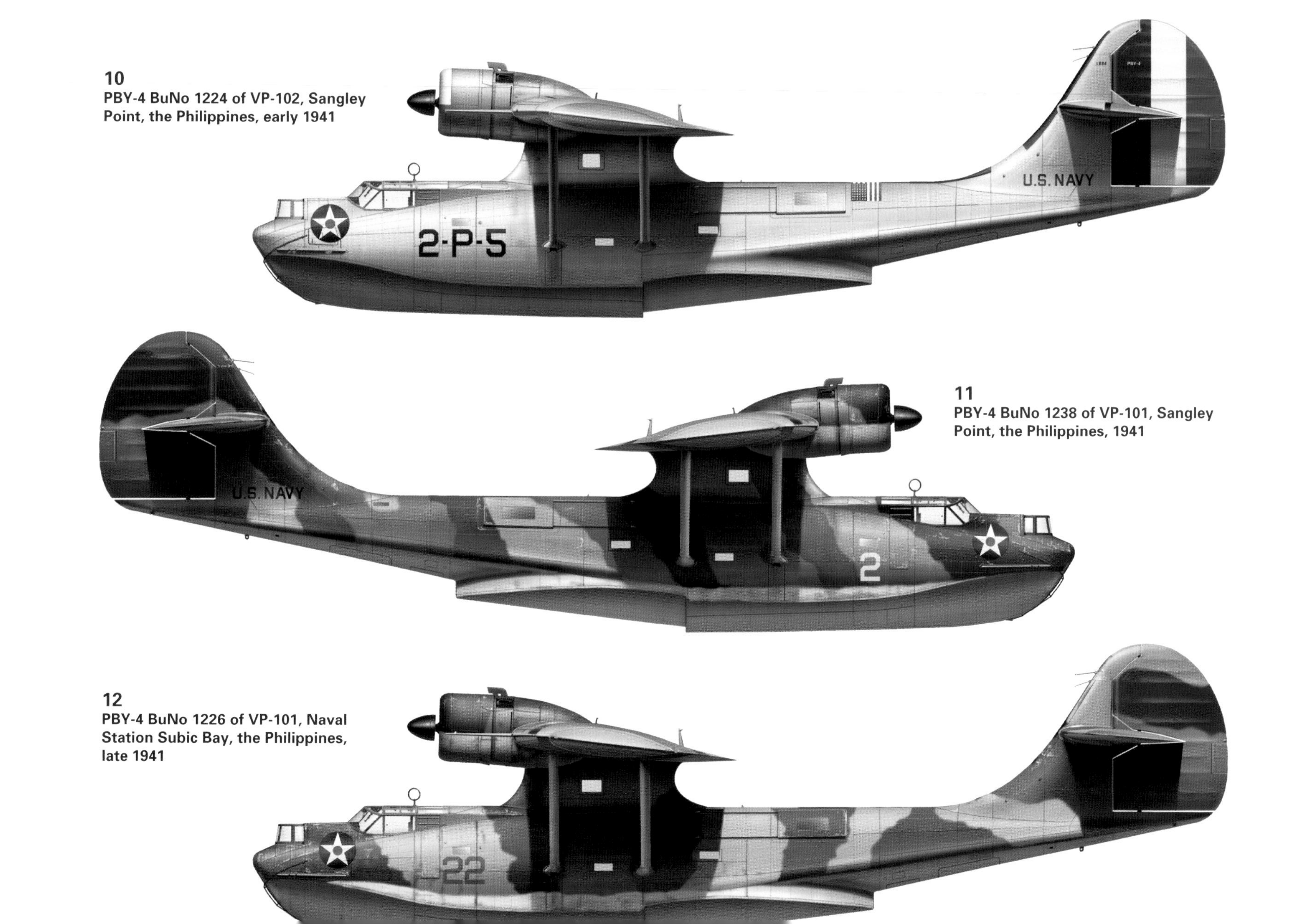

10
PBY-4 BuNo 1224 of VP-102, Sangley Point, the Philippines, early 1941

11
PBY-4 BuNo 1238 of VP-101, Sangley Point, the Philippines, 1941

12
PBY-4 BuNo 1226 of VP-101, Naval Station Subic Bay, the Philippines, late 1941

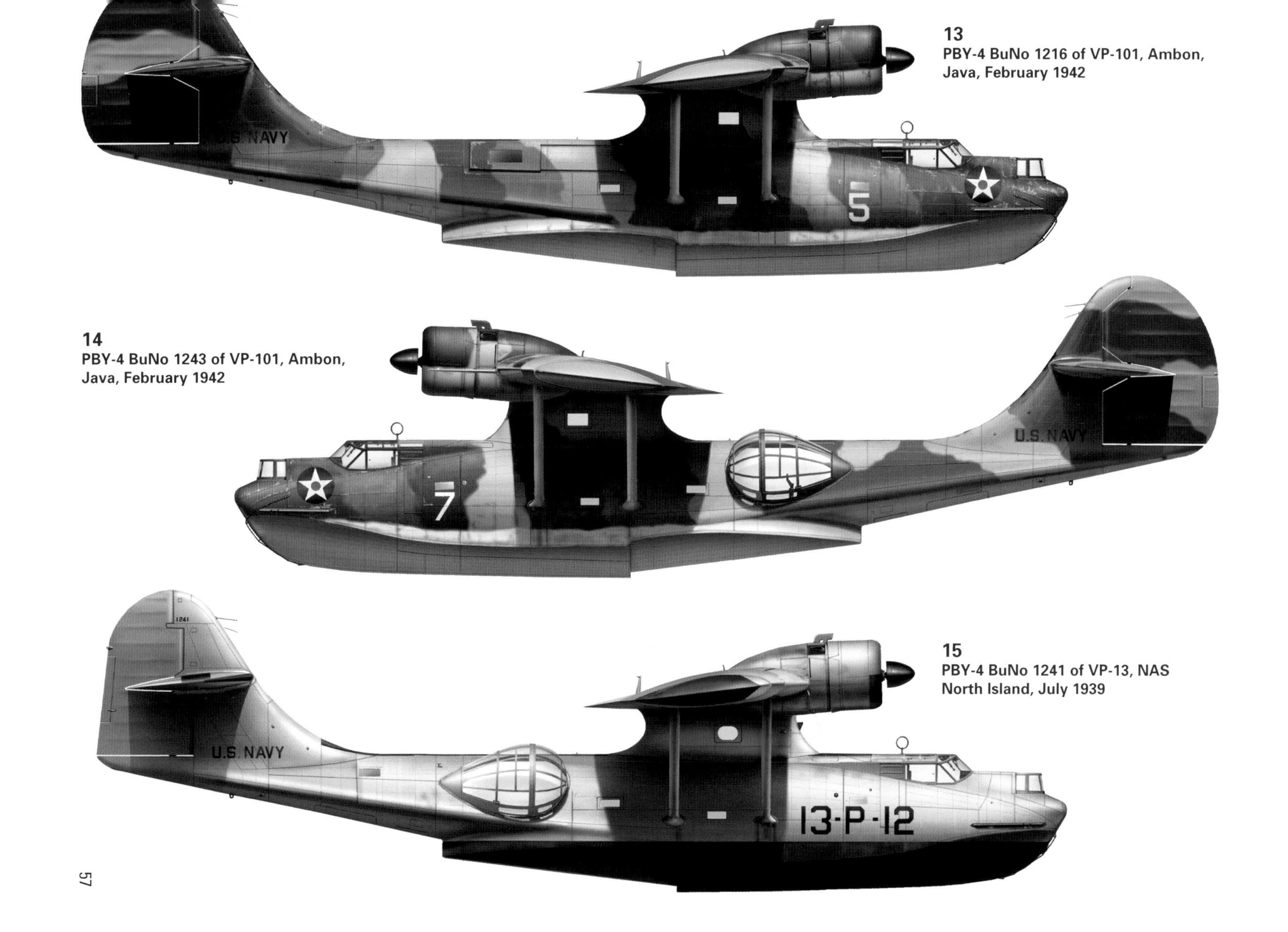

13
PBY-4 BuNo 1216 of VP-101, Ambon, Java, February 1942

14
PBY-4 BuNo 1243 of VP-101, Ambon, Java, February 1942

15
PBY-4 BuNo 1241 of VP-13, NAS North Island, July 1939

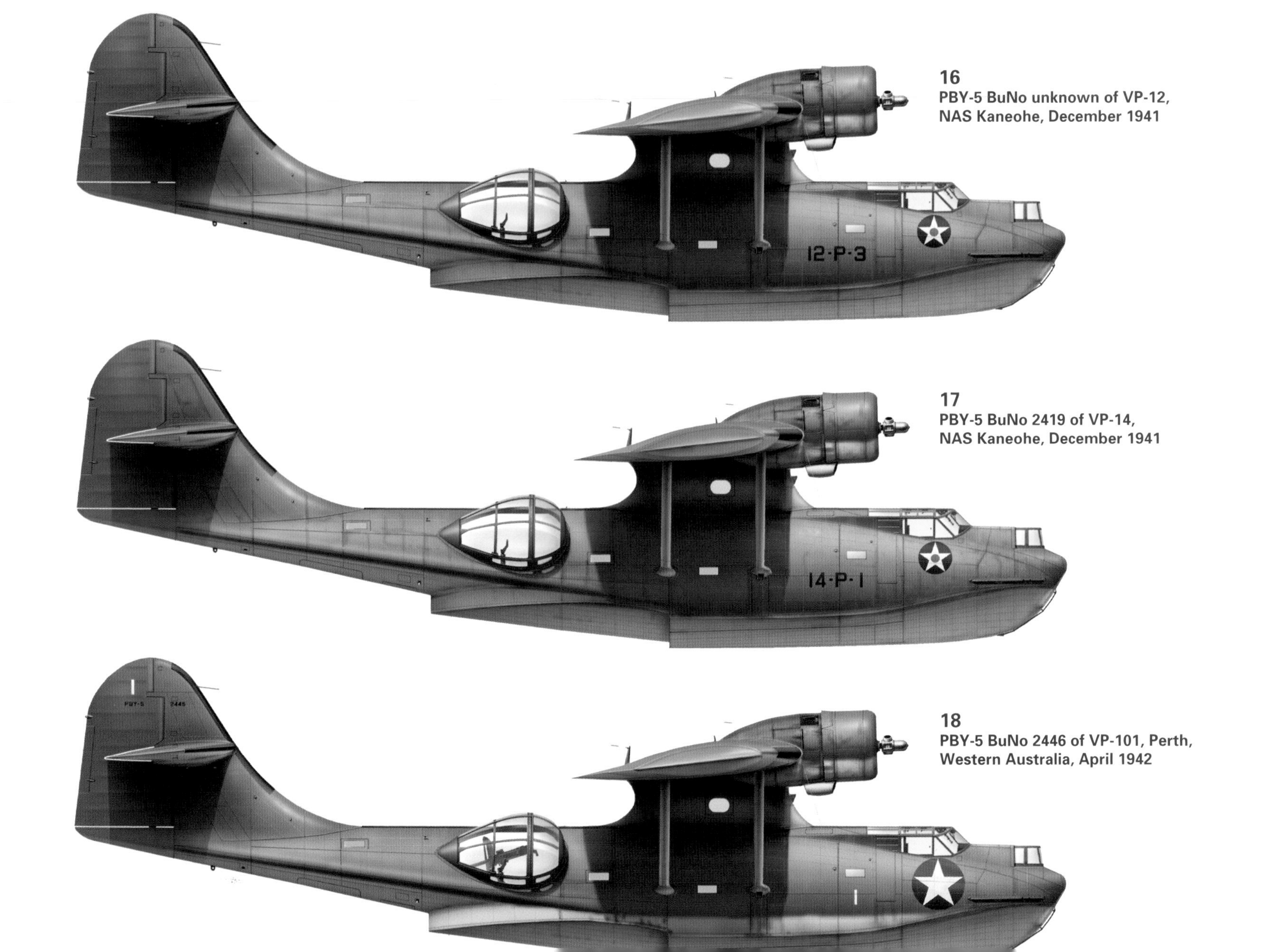

16
PBY-5 BuNo unknown of VP-12,
NAS Kaneohe, December 1941

17
PBY-5 BuNo 2419 of VP-14,
NAS Kaneohe, December 1941

18
PBY-5 BuNo 2446 of VP-101, Perth,
Western Australia, April 1942

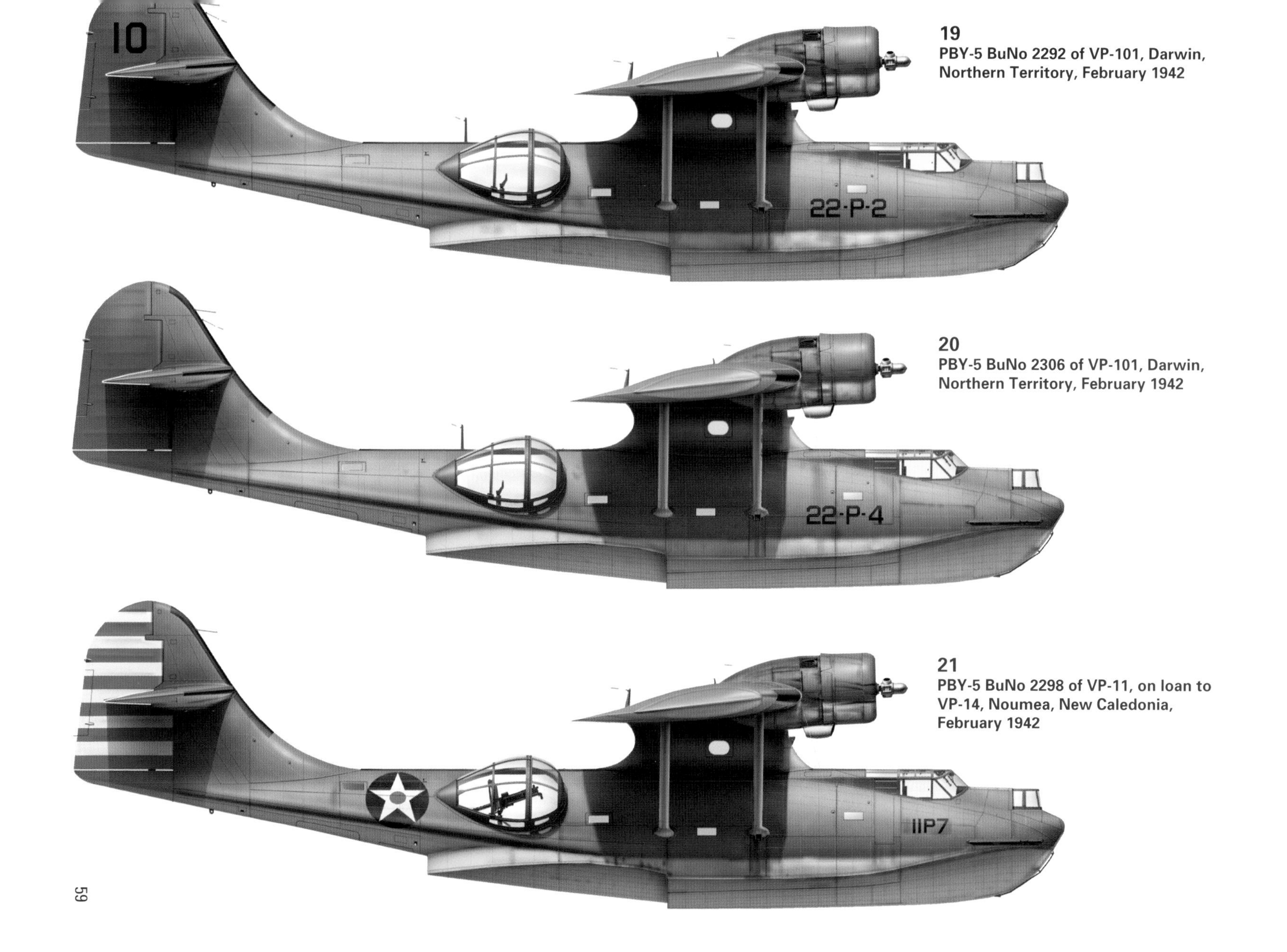

19
PBY-5 BuNo 2292 of VP-101, Darwin, Northern Territory, February 1942

20
PBY-5 BuNo 2306 of VP-101, Darwin, Northern Territory, February 1942

21
PBY-5 BuNo 2298 of VP-11, on loan to VP-14, Noumea, New Caledonia, February 1942

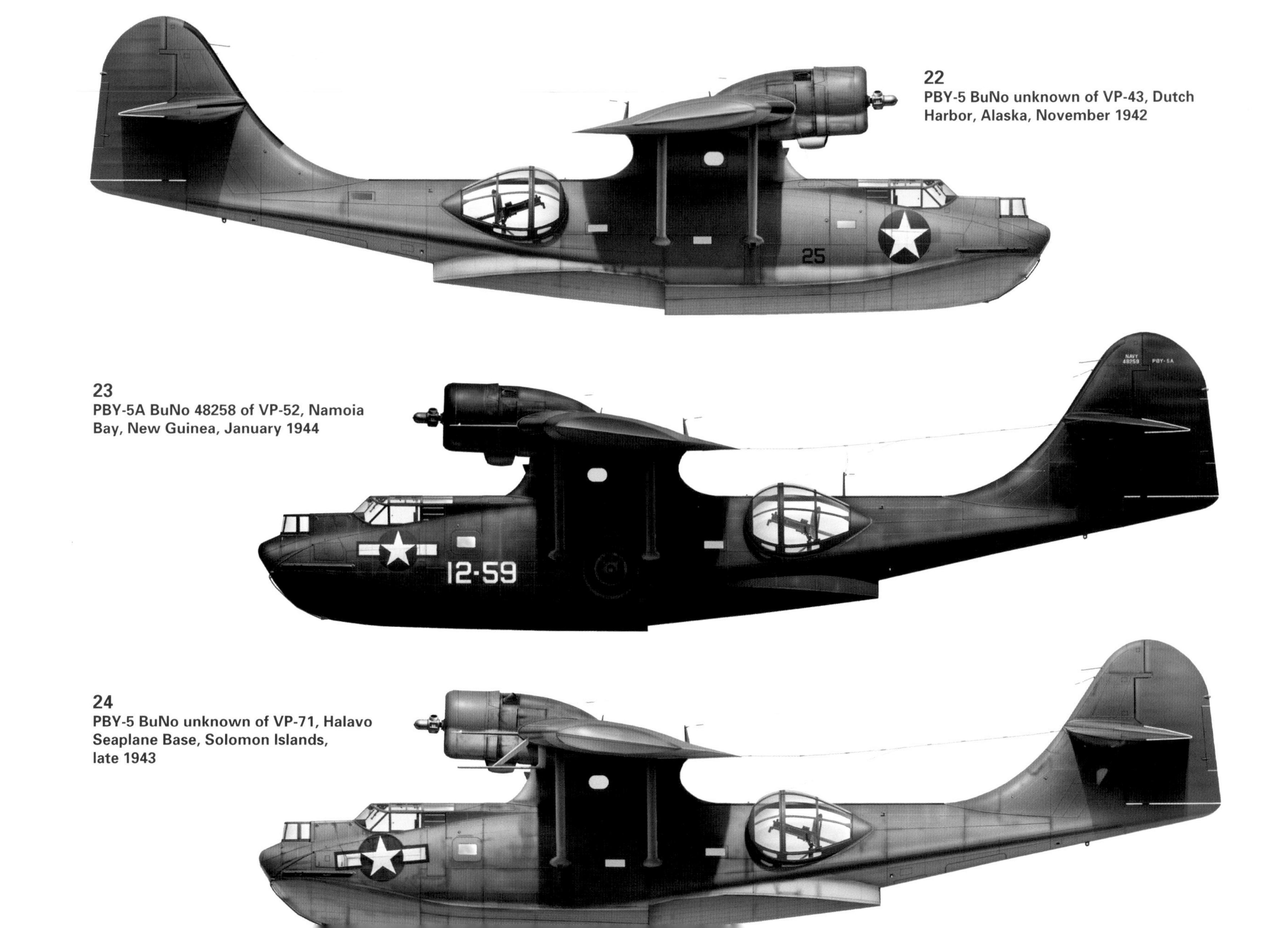

22
PBY-5 BuNo unknown of VP-43, Dutch Harbor, Alaska, November 1942

23
PBY-5A BuNo 48258 of VP-52, Namoia Bay, New Guinea, January 1944

24
PBY-5 BuNo unknown of VP-71, Halavo Seaplane Base, Solomon Islands, late 1943

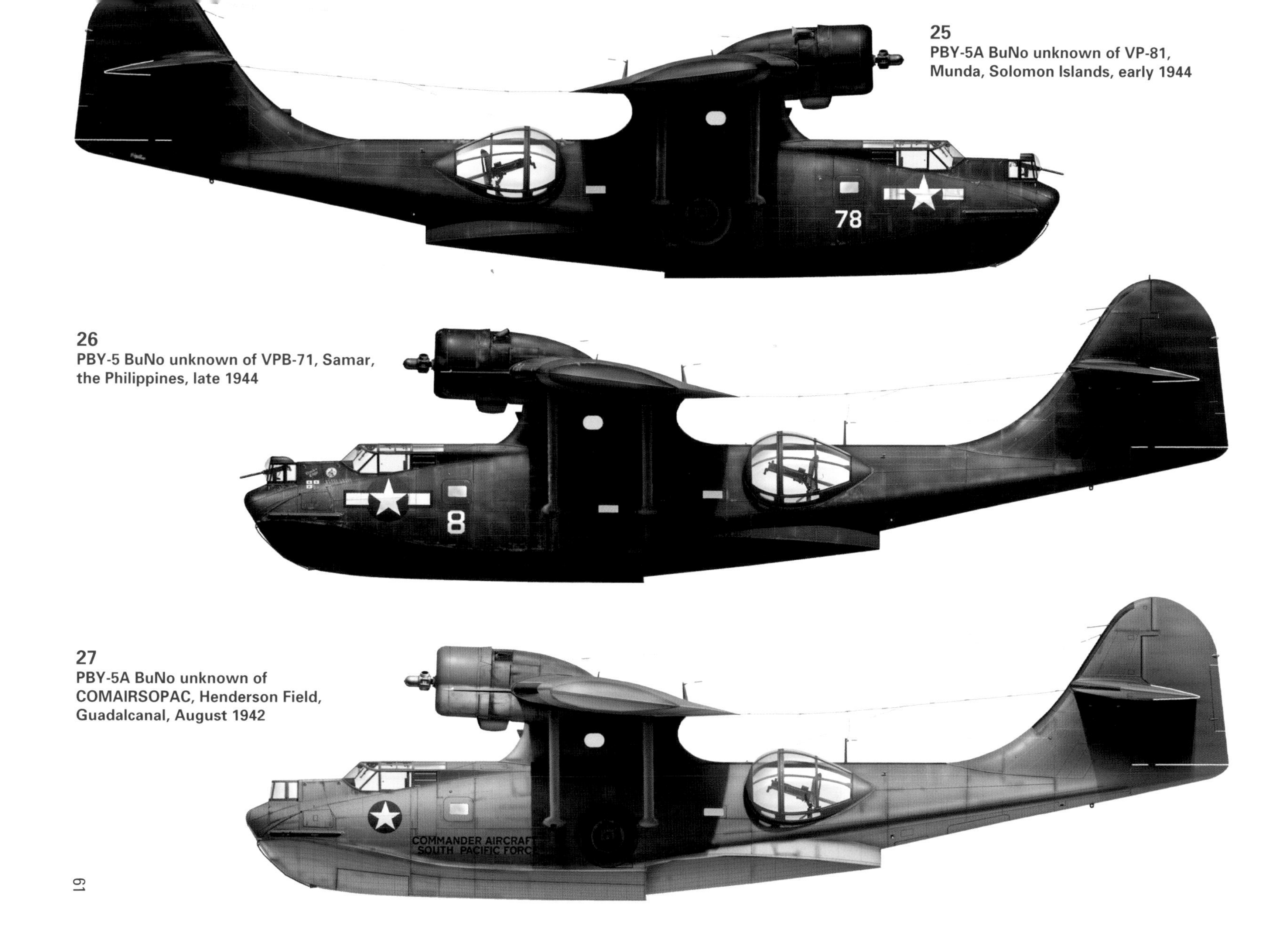

25
PBY-5A BuNo unknown of VP-81, Munda, Solomon Islands, early 1944

26
PBY-5 BuNo unknown of VPB-71, Samar, the Philippines, late 1944

27
PBY-5A BuNo unknown of COMAIRSOPAC, Henderson Field, Guadalcanal, August 1942

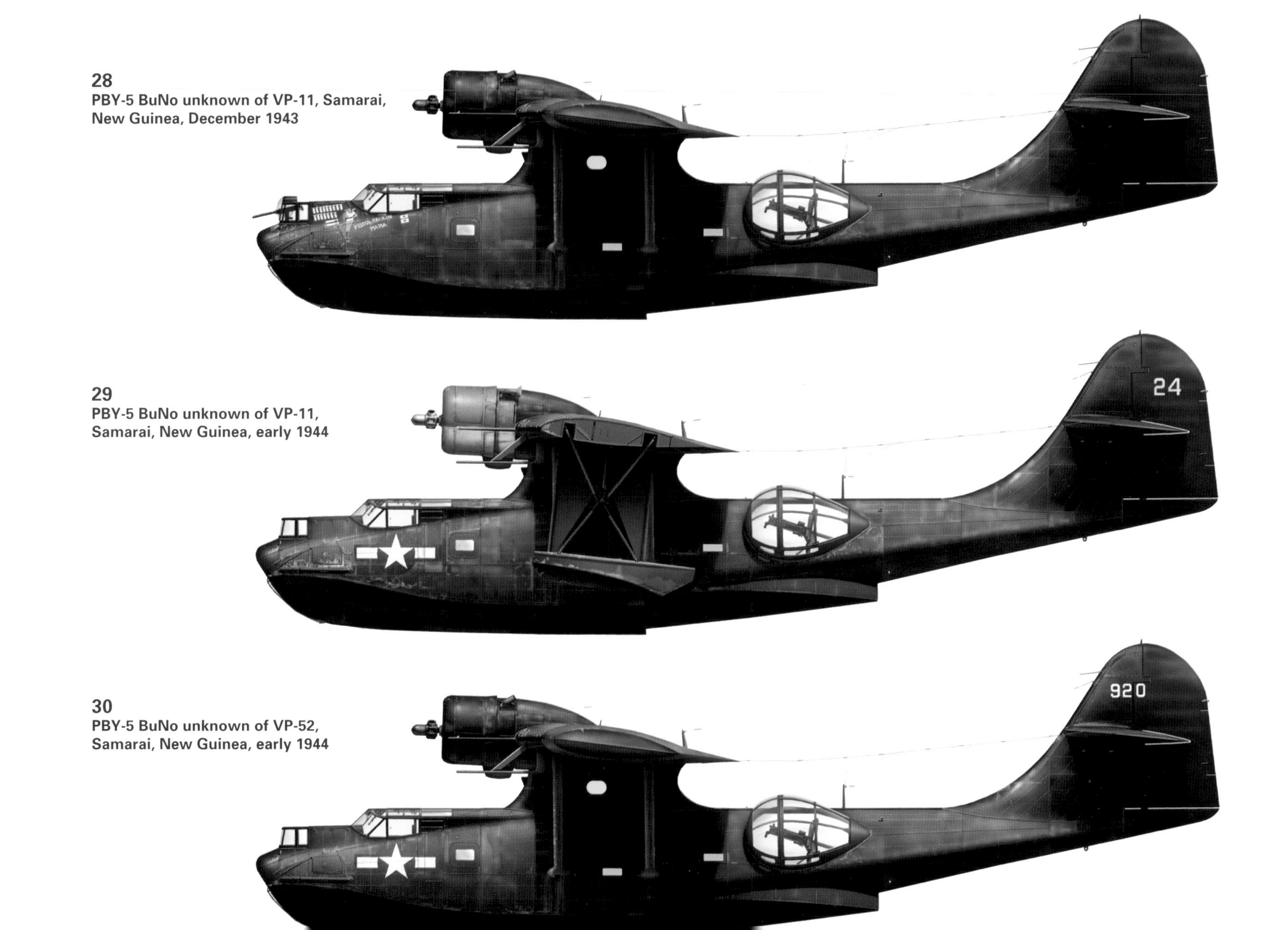

28
PBY-5 BuNo unknown of VP-11, Samarai, New Guinea, December 1943

29
PBY-5 BuNo unknown of VP-11, Samarai, New Guinea, early 1944

30
PBY-5 BuNo unknown of VP-52, Samarai, New Guinea, early 1944

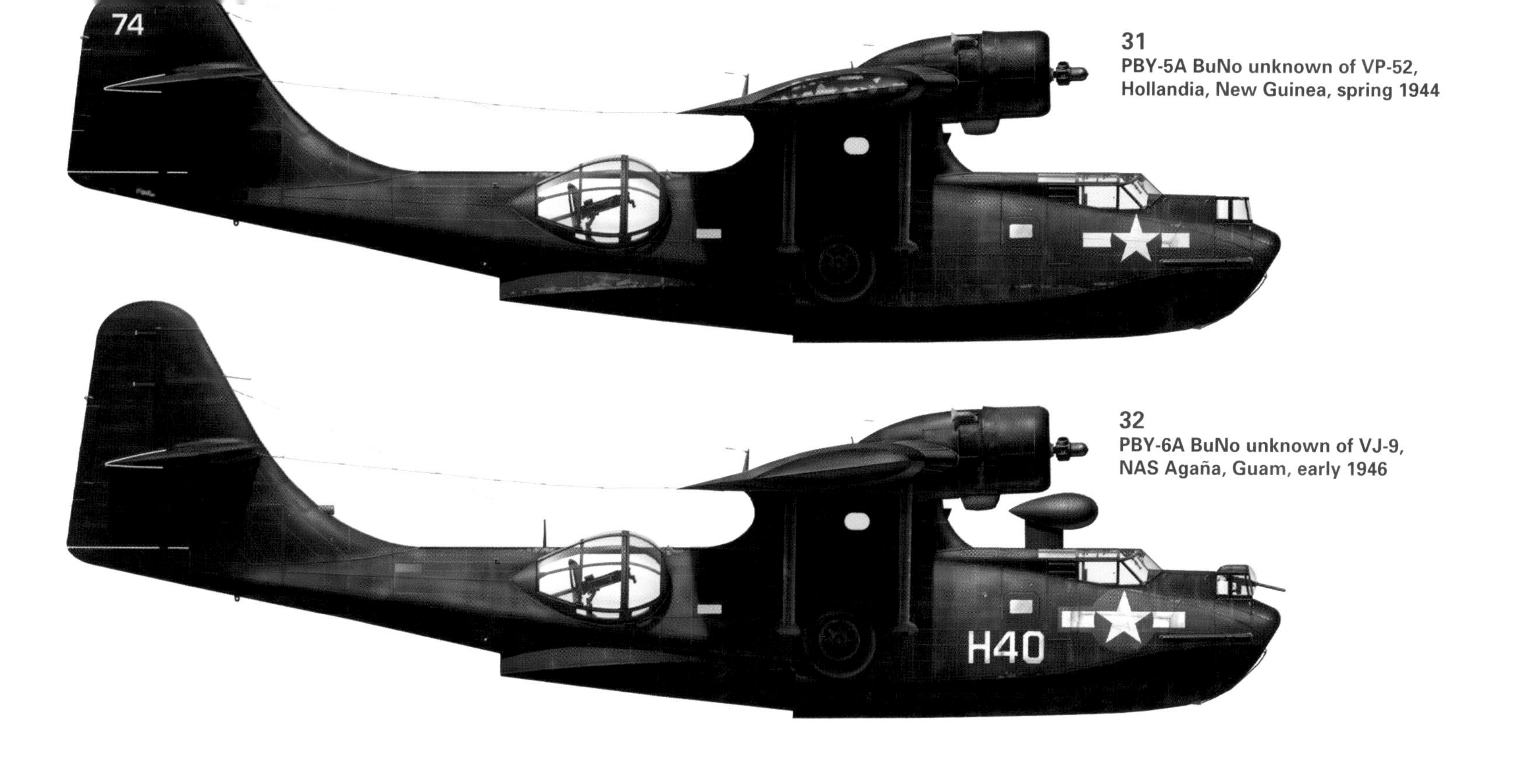

31
**PBY-5A BuNo unknown of VP-52,
Hollandia, New Guinea, spring 1944**

32
**PBY-6A BuNo unknown of VJ-9,
NAS Agaña, Guam, early 1946**

1943

In January 1943, four wings, controlling a dozen PBY-5/5A-equipped VP squadrons, faced the Japanese in the Pacific. FAW 1 was operating in the Solomons, FAW 10 in the East Indies and New Guinea, FAW 2 in Hawaii and FAW 4 in the Aleutians. Three more squadrons (VP-11, VP-45 and VP-91) were refitting, training and working up on the west coast, and a further trio (VP-33, VP-34 and VP-52) in the Atlantic had been alerted that they would soon transfer to the Pacific.

VP operations in the South and Southwest Pacific were distinctively different, with FAW 10 and VP-101 in the latter theatre continuing to probe and harass enemy forces deep into the occupied East Indies. In the South Pacific, PBY units focused their attention on the Solomons.

FAW 1, with its staff embarked in *Curtiss* at Espiritu Santo, mustered six squadrons of PBYs at the start of the year, but VP-11 left for California in February for re-equipment. VP-72, with 16 PBY-5As, went ashore to Henderson Field at the same time. Due to the ferocity of the incessant air combat in the Solomons, both VP-24 at Espiritu Santo and VP-72 were continuously employed flying air sea rescue (ASR) missions. When Guadalcanal was finally declared secured on 9 February, FAW 1 moved forward from Espiritu Santo to Henderson Field on 1 March. VP-23 arrived on Guadalcanal to help share the load in June.

Across 'the Slot' on Tulagi, the SeaBees had firstly repaired and were now expanding the small seaplane station on the island. This facility would eventually take over the entire Halavo peninsula on Florida Island. Between the PBY-5As working from Henderson Field and the PBY-5s based in the sheltered bay off Halavo, the Guadalcanal/Tulagi complex provided Catalina coverage for the entire Solomons chain.

Long-range patrols may have seemed mundane to most aviators in-theatre, but the PBY's proven ability to patrol far and wide made the aircraft worth its weight in gold. Its crews would be the first to spot enemy fleet movements, and, conversely, negative reports indicating that such and such a sector was clear were often just as valuable.

VP-44 arrived in the Solomons with its PBY-5s in mid-January and picked up some of the pressing ASR duties. VP-54, which would soon expand VP-12's clandestine 'Black Cat' work (see Chapter 8), flew in a few weeks later, while VP-71 and VP-91 both returned home in March. The latter unit would then spend the next four months reforming and training up with fresh personnel on new aircraft.

VP-81's PBY-5A 'Black Cats' rest during daylight hours at Henderson Field, on Guadalcanal, in late 1943. There were 20 VP units operating in the Pacific at the time this photograph was taken

Australian technicians at the RAAF's No 1 Flying Boat Repair Base at Lake Boga, near Swan Hill, Victoria, overhauled and reworked both Commonwealth and US Navy Catalinas. Here, airframe reworking is being carried out in the open while a recently-completed US Navy PBY-5 is readied for take-off from Lake Boga in the distance (*Dave's Warbirds*)

By mid-1943, the Pacific battlefield was shifting northward, leaving PBYs to transit between Hawaii and Espiritu Santo or Guadalcanal with little chance of encountering enemy aeroplanes en route.

The number of PBY-equipped VP units in the Pacific surged to 20 during the second half of 1943, with 13 of them being committed to frontline operations and the remaining seven (VP-12, VP-24, VP-43, VP-44, VP-53, VP-62 and VP-81) spending time with the Pacific Fleet prior to refitting and training on new aircraft types.

One organisational change that affected all PBY squadrons in the Pacific during the course of the year was the implementation of the Patrol Aviation Service Unit (PATSU) concept, which separated the squadron's flight crew personnel and aeroplanes from the groundcrew. The latter now formed up into generic groundcrew and maintenance support teams independent of specific squadrons. PATSU-1 worked at Henderson Field, with another numbered unit based at Halavo. Both teams serviced, maintained and acted as groundcrew for all and any PBYs present at the bases. Others followed, the PATSUs in effect being seaplane tenders based ashore. This innovative idea was simplicity itself, and allowed great flexibility in moving units about quickly to meet changing requirements.

In advanced areas, and for tactical purposes, the tenders, large or small, continued to service PBYs wherever they operated. When aircraft needed overhauling, rather than maintenance and repair, this was done by RAAF facilities at Rathmines and Lake Boga, as well as others in rear areas.

Serviceability rates were put to the test in the Southwest Pacific theatre when Allied forces began to exert pressure on the Japanese stronghold of Rabaul. The enemy positions here, and in surrounding areas, were formidable, but not impregnable. The enemy, too, depended on seaborne supplies and support, and the Japanese were finding that it was becoming ever harder to maintain links via the sea as air superiority changed hands.

The US move northward towards Rabaul advanced further in July and August following the taking of the New Georgia islands. Like the fighting in the Solomons, this was a tough campaign. The airfield at Munda Point was an early and important objective, and it was seized on 5 August.

In advance of this operation, PBYs had flown in a team of Recon Marines to thoroughly scout the islands, and their intelligence reports formed the basis for assault planning. There were several landings on New Georgia itself (on 30 June), and then on the Kula Gulf at Enogai Inlet, Rice Anchorage and Biaroko (on 5 July), where the destroyers USS *Strong* and USS *Nicholas* provided artillery support fire to the Marines ashore. The following three weeks saw a brutal battle fought by US forces as they struggled to oust the entrenched enemy.

USS *Wright* anchored in a New Georgia inlet virtually on the frontline soon after the invasion and supported the PBYs of VP-72.

PATSU 1-1's homebuilt jeep on Guadalcanal sits in front of a PBY-5A 'Black Cat' undergoing a landing gear check. The PATSUs greatly improved the level of maintenance and repair work carried out on VP aircraft from 1943 onwards (*Warren Larsen*)

To the southeast, PBYs of FAW 1 at Henderson Field and elsewhere contributed significantly to the campaign, although in a supporting role for the many land-based fighter and bomber units that were now carrying the battle to the enemy. The innovative 'Black Cat' operations, detailed in Chapter 8, were proving very effective, and most nights one or more PBYs would prowl Japanese-held areas north of Guadalcanal.

The intensity of the air combat in this theatre also meant that Dumbo ASR crews had steady, and critical, work too.

And the Catalina could still perform its traditional anti-submarine role when called on, as was the case on 15 September when a VP-23 PBY, flown by Lt W J Geritz and crew, helped flush out the enemy submarine RO-101 south of San Christobal. The vessel, which had previously been attacked by the destroyer USS *Saufley*, was struck by one of two depth charges dropped from the Catalina and subsequently sank with all hands.

NEW GUINEA

FAW 17 was established in Brisbane, Queensland, on 15 September 1943 to better direct naval tender and shore-based VP squadrons supporting the New Guinea campaign. Like FAW 10, FAW 17 worked directly for the Commander of Aircraft Seventh Fleet, and its units flew exclusively in the New Guinea area, leaving the Solomons to FAW 1.

Seabees built a complete naval air station at Palm Island, just north of Brisbane, and aircraft could also be overhauled here – it was kept busy reworking PBYs well into 1944, when the front moved too far north for it to continue to be effective in this role. VP-101 was the first unit to move permanently into the New Guinea area, the squadron arriving in July to operate from USS *San Pablo*, anchored in Namoia Bay. This quickly proved to be an excellent anchorage for advanced base operations.

In addition to flying combat patrols, VP-101 also undertook re-supply and medical evacuation runs into the New Guinea highlands, where the PBYs would land on the Sepik River in support of Australian troops. The unit would also pull these men out of the area when the number of enemy soldiers in the immediate locale grew too large to handle. Airlifting these troops saved much blood and sweat for the Australian infantrymen.

On 31 December FAW 17 left Brisbane for the new seaplane base at Samarai, near Namoia Bay. Following the Allied landings at Finschafen (23 September) and Cape Gloucester (28 Dececember), the Solomons Sea south of the New Guinea–New Britain 'gap' was entirely lost to Japan. Keen to exploit this situation, FAW 17 sent *San Pablo* forward to provide advanced base operations from Langemak Bay, off Finschafen.

CENTRAL PACIFIC CAMPAIGN

Immediately after the attack on Pearl Harbor, Kaneohe-based squadrons began sending dets of PBYs to patrol from the island groups along the ferry route skirting the Gilbert Islands, which the Japanese had invaded in January 1942. Daily, PBYs would fly from Palmyra to Canton, then on to the Ellice Islands, Tonga and finally Fiji.

On 30 November 1943 the Marine Corps landed on Tarawa and other islands in the Gilberts (Operation *Galvanic*), which were then used as a springboard for further advances in the Pacific. By the time this amphibious assault was launched, the organisation of US forces had significantly evolved since the taking of Guadalcanal 15 months earlier. Now, the US Fifth Fleet had a significant number of large carriers ready to overwhelm the enemy from the air, while aircraft from smaller escort carriers provided direct air support for the Marines ashore. Battleships and cruisers were also available to provide direct fire bombardments.

Task Force 57, commanded by Rear Admiral John C Hoover, was the land- and tender-based air support element of *Galvanic*. Its units, operating ASR and reconnaissance patrol aircraft, were primarily based in the Ellice Islands at Funafuti harbour. TG 57.3 controlled two squadrons of twelve Catalinas, with VP-53's PBY-5As flying from a shore base and VP-72's PBY-5s on the tenders *Curtiss*, *Mackinac* and *Swan*.

Also included in Task Group 57.3 was VB-108's 12 PB4Y-1 Liberators, as well as two squadrons of PV-1 Venturas and photo-reconnaissance unit VD-3, again flying Liberators. The long-range photo work and most of the anti-shipping strikes were performed by the newer, faster aircraft, leaving the PBYs to carry out sector search patrols and ASR.

The muscle in Admiral Hoover's organisation was provided by the 90 USAAF B-24s that would pay a visit to every Japanese position within range. The dark days of 1941-42 were now behind US forces in the Pacific, which were on the move against the enemy. The PBYs were still very much involved in frontline operations, however, and within a few months the Fifth Fleet was getting ready to help with the seizure of the Marshall Islands. Task Group 57.3 PBYs continued to undertake the long-range scouting and patrol work throughout this period, and the force was joined by yet another US Navy Liberator squadron (VB-109), as well as five squadrons of dive-bombers.

Having held the line in the Pacific for so long, the PBY was now being supplanted, and would eventually be replaced, by a new breed of land-based and amphibious aircraft. Amongst the latter was Martin's PBM Mariner, the examples of which arrived in the Pacific in February 1943.

As previously mentioned, higher performance PV-1s also began reaching the frontline during the course of 1943, with Seattle-based VP-42 being amongst the first PBY units to make the transition as VB-135. At Kaneohe, several experienced VP-14 pilots and crews were detailed away to help form VB-102 at San Diego, and half the VP-71 crews followed to help establish VB-104 – both units were equipped with PB4Y-1s. The two squadrons then filled out with replacement crews and new aircraft and returned to regular operations. In such ways the emerging VB squadrons, with newer, faster and more heavily armed bombers, drew upon the experience of the often bloodied PBY veterans.

NORTH PACIFIC

In the Aleutians, the PBYs remained critical for island patrols, anti-submarine operations and ASR, whilst their numerous flights carrying mail, supplies and personnel were no less valuable throughout 1943. In January of that year VP-61 was ordered to bring its PBY-5As forward from Seattle to Kodiak, before replacing VP-42 at Otter Point – the latter unit returned to Seattle. FAW 4 also moved west to the new airfield on Adak on 15 March, which was already home to VP-62's PBY-5As.

A major enemy effort to re-supply its troops in the Aleutians was thwarted altogether by the Battle of the Kommandorskis on 26 March, which was a long, drawn out, surface action fought some 200 miles west of Attu. The enemy's naval commander, shadowed by PBYs, and anxious not to be exposed to land-based bombers, failed to complete his mission to move supplies into the occupied islands. Thereafter, Japanese efforts changed their focus from invasion to evacuation. US air power, and in particular the PBYs, had had a telling effect on the conflict in the Aleutians.

A VP-45 PBY departs Attu in August 1943, its tender, USS *Casco*, moored immediately behind the Catalina. This unit was supported by the vessel at Attu from July through to September 1943

The American/Canadian effort to rid the theatre of enemy troops culminated in the assault on occupied Attu on 13 May. VP-61 moved from Adak to Attu's newly-bulldozed strip at Alexei Point on 7 June and immediately began pushing its patrols further west in search of the retreating enemy. No trace of the Japanese was found, however. Elsewhere, VP-43 and VP-62 returned to Seattle for fresh aircraft shortly after Attu had been taken, and in late June PV-1-equipped VB-135 and VB-136 reported to FAW 4 to augment the PBYs.

By mid-1943, the enemy was firmly on the run in the Aleutians. PBYs from VP-45 and VP-61 were flying long patrols in search of Japanese fleet units attempting to stop the rout, but no vessels came. On 15 August Kiska was found to be vacant, its previous occupants having abandoned it unnoticed. By then PBY-5As and PV-1s flying from Alexis Point had begun to push patrols well to the west, with VP-45 launching its first reconnaissance missions to probe Japanese positions in the northern Kurile Islands, 700 miles away off the tip of Soviet Kamchatka. FAW 4 reported VP-45's results and findings, and very soon CINCPAC at Pearl directed a steady campaign of photo-reconnaissance and bombing missions to keep track of and harass enemy activity in the Kuriles.

FAW 4 assigned the bombing missions to the PV-1 squadrons, as the Lockheed aircraft was faster and better able to handle defending fighters than the PBY-5A – VB-136 flew the first 'Empire Express' mission on 16 November. Without bombs, however, the Catalina had a greater range and more loiter time over the target. VP-43 moved into Attu in October, allowing VP-45 and VP-61 to withdraw. The new unit launched a series of opportune photo-reconnaissance missions to the northern Kurile Islands on 20 December that soon confirmed that the enemy was not present in strength here either, thus ending the Japanese threat to Alaska.

VP-61's PBY-5 'Boat 72' takes on fuel from a seaplane tender somewhere in the Aleutians in early 1943. VP-42, VP-43 and VP-62 all operated PBY-5As with PatWing/FAW 4 in this area at the time, but only VP-61 used non-amphibious PBY-5s (*Dave's Warbirds*)

1944

In January 1944, the US Navy still had 16 Catalina-equipped VP units in the Pacific. Five were flying amphibian PBY-5As, with four more (including VP-1 and VP-3, again with PBY-5As) refitting on the west coast. Units were flying patrols from Attu, in the Aleutians, to Exmouth Gulf, on Australia's distant west coast. In addition, at NAS Kaneohe, FAW 2 had the first two Pacific PBM squadrons (VP-202 and VP-216) undergoing advanced combat training and running patrols from Oahu.

In the Southwest and South Pacific theatres, Allied forces were very much on the offensive. On 29 February, the Admiralty Islands were seized. Amongst the territory captured was the island of Manus, with its excellent airfield at Lorengau and the fine seaplane and fleet anchorage at Seeadler harbour. Emirau Island, in the St Matthias group, also fell under Allied control on 17 March. These offensives isolated Japanese forces in the Bismarck Islands, leaving strongholds such as Rabaul bypassed and cut off from the rest of the Empire until the end of the war.

FAW 17 at Samarai orchestrated the many PBY patrols and raids along the coast during these campaigns in early 1944, flying in Army Rangers to reconnoitre Manus Island in preparation for the landings. Following the seizure of this new territory, Catalina squadrons and detachments advanced rapidly to keep the pressure on the enemy. Follow-up landings then came in quick succession at Hollandia (21-24 April) and Biak (27 May), allowing American and Australian troops to move smartly up along the northwestern New Guinea coast beyond Biak to Middleburg Island and Morotai, in preparation for the retaking of the Philippines.

Within the Southwest Pacific theatre's Seventh Fleet, Commander FAW 17, Commodore T S Combs, was 'double-hatted' as Commander Task Force 73 in charge of all US Navy land- and tender-based aviation units. These squadrons, and their locations, within this organisation routinely changed between March and August 1944, thus illustrating the flexible and evolving nature of this campaign. The commodore was both CTF 73 and also CTG 73.1, commanding the Seeadler Harbour Group in the Admiralties, which included VP-33 (a 'Black Cat' unit) in USS *Tangier* and VP-52 in USS *San Pablo* and USS *Heron*, each with 13 PBY-5s, and also VB-106 with 11 PB4Y-1s ashore at Lorengau Field.

Cdr W O Gallery was CTG 73.2, which was operating from USS *Half Moon* and other tenders in Langemak Bay, off Finschafen, with VP-34's ten PBY-5s and the Catalinas of both Nos 11 and 20 Sqns of the RAAF. By June these units had begun moving up the coast in the wake of Allied advances.

Ex-*Bird* class minesweeper USS *Heron* served for many years pre-war on the Asiatic Station tending seaplanes. It continued to perform this role throughout the war in the Pacific, with vessels of this size proving to be handy, efficient tenders for PBY detachments operating for short periods at remote anchorages (*US Navy*)

From Perth, VP-11 continued its long-range harassment missions into the Dutch islands from advanced bases such as Exmouth Gulf.

Elsewhere, South Pacific forces focused sharply on the neutralisation of cut-off Japanese troops in the Bismarck Islands, with Rabaul being the primary focus of its attention. The aerial campaign against these centres was in full swing by 1944, with units working from advanced bases in Bougainville and the Green Islands (captured on 16 February). Solomon Islands Air Defense (AirSols) attack squadrons were now literally on Rabaul's doorstep, and they flew missions against the beleaguered Japanese stronghold literally round the clock. 'Black Cat' and Dumbo operations were also undertaken on a continuous basis.

On Guadalcanal, FAW 1 controlled VP-14 and VP-71 at Halavo, VP-72 with PBY-5As at Funafuti, VP-81 ('Black Cats') with more PBY-5As at Henderson Field, VP-91 (running long-range patrols and convoy escort from Espiritu Santo) in USS *Chandeleur*, and a det on USS *Mackinac* at Suva. VP-81 subsequently relieved VP-71 at Halavo, before moving to 'Piva Yoke' field at Empress Augusta Bay, in Bougainville. 'Black Cats' were now closer than ever to Rabaul and Kaveing, and the enemy felt the pinch. VP-14 duly moved forward to a tender at Hathorne Sound, New Georgia, and by June it had a det in the Green Islands.

Fresh from San Diego, VP-54 ('Black Cats') joined VP-91 ('Black Cats') at Halavo in late March, and within 30 days the latter unit had sent detachments forward to the Treasuries, in the Green Islands, and to Emirau. The Japanese at Rabaul were now surrounded by PBYs!

CENTRAL PACIFIC CAMPAIGN

Following the capture of the Gilbert and Marshall islands in the central Pacific, FAW 2 sent both VP-72 and land-based VB units to the area. PBYs still participated, and excelled, in the critical Dumbo ASR mission, but long-range search and attack tasks were now performed by new VB squadrons equipped with PB4Y-1s. The Consolidated four-engined bomber could fly nearly as far as a PBY but at a much greater speed, and with a bigger bomb load too. The aircraft also had sufficient defensive firepower to take care of itself should enemy fighters be encountered.

VP squadrons in this theatre also provided detachments to perform ASR support for Third and Fifth Fleet carriers operating in the region. Unlike in 1942, when *Enterprise* and *Saratoga* were the sole 'flattops' in the area, there were now four task groups, each with three or four new aircraft carriers assigned. These were crammed full off new-generation aircraft such as the F6F Hellcat, TBF/TBM Avenger and SB2C Helldiver. The US Navy now went pretty much where it pleased, and although scouting for enemy fleet movements remained a high priority task, far-reaching land-based VP/VB aircraft performed this mission.

In 1941-42, the PBY had often been the only source of reconnaissance and scouting information on the enemy, but by 1944 technological advances in several fields initially augmented, and then began replacing the Catalinas in this mission. Radar, the complex field of communications intelligence (traffic analysis, direction finding, cryptanalysis and codebreaking of radio traffic) and the arrival of faster, better armed, higher performance aircraft effectively rendered the PBY redundant in the scouting mission.

VP crews served as the eyes of the Pacific Fleet for much of World War 2. Locating the enemy at sea was the Catalina's job, and its reports were frequently crucial to the success of a battle. In between, it was just more routine, endless ocean, with crews typically patrolling on their own (*Dave's Warbirds*)

Nevertheless, the Catalina's work would continue right through to VJ-Day in the Pacific, and even beyond. The aircraft did not make many headlines with its utility and ASR patrols, often performed in less active areas, but mail from home was reaching remote outposts – often flown in by a PBY – and morale was up.

And outposts did not come more remote than those in the Aleutians, where the Catalina found gainful employment through to war's end. VP-43 had departed the theatre in February 1944 to re-equip with PV-1s as VP-139. While land-based bombers continued to raid the Kuriles, the PBYs at Attu and Adak handled the ASR and general utility work.

Meanwhile, in Hawaii, and on the west coast of the USA, PBY units continued to transition onto more modern aircraft. One such squadron was VP-81, which, after months of successful 'Black Cat' operations in the Solomons, was relieved on 1 June and sent home to convert onto the PB4Y-2 Privateer – VP-14 followed soon afterwards.

In March 1944 the last PBY-5 left the San Diego assembly line, even as the very first of the highly modified, and navalised, Privateers rolled out of the same plant and were assigned to waiting US Navy squadrons. This was not the end of Catalina production, however, for Consolidated's brand new New Orleans factory was just getting into gear, producing a solitary PBY-5 in April and seven more in June.

PV-1s and PB4Y-1s were well established in the Pacific by mid-1944 when the PBM Mariner finally made its first forward deployments to the theatre. Eight squadrons of PBMs were subsequently sent to the Pacific, where they initially operated alongside the PBY in the ASR, patrol and re-supply roles. However, when the US Navy established dedicated ASR squadrons (VH) later that year, they primarily received PBM-3s – VH-2 was unique in receiving Boeing-built PB2B-1 Catalinas.

FIGHTING IN THE SOUTH PACIFIC

The PBYs remained dominant in the South Pacific for much of 1944, with VP-54 searching for targets at night and VP-71 conducting ASR by day. The VP ranks were reduced by one unit on 30 July, however, when VP-12 was withdrawn – it would not return to combat. VP-44 and VP-91 continued operations from Green Islands, flying both 'Black Cat' and ASR missions, but VP-23 and VP-72 were moved forward to new bases in the Marshalls at Eniwetok and Ebeye to provide dedicated Dumbo services to the many shore-based fighter and bomber squadrons moving into the islands from the Gilberts and Hawaii.

By now the writing was on the wall for the PBY, for in addition to VP-12 being pulled out, VP-72 and VP-91 were also ordered to return to the US for refit. The transferring out of these units were the early drawdowns that victory in the Pacific would ultimately bring.

FAW 2's recently-arrived PBM units found themselves very much in the thick of the action in the central Pacific supporting the Marianas Islands landings on Saipan (15 June), Guam (21 July) and Tinian (24 July), as well as the Battle of the Philippine Sea (19 June). VP-16's PBM-3s mounted patrols from Saipan, supported by USS *Pocomoke* and USS *Onslow*, as well as PATSUs established on each of the islands.

Commander FAW 1 still had a considerable number of PBYs scattered all over the South Pacific, primarily aimed at supporting the offensive against Rabaul. In order to be closer to the action, the wing's commander shifted his HQ to Woendi, in Dutch New Guinea, on 11 September. FAW 1 would now call the new tender USS *Hamlin* home. Once in-theatre, it set about assembling a force of VP aircraft (primarily PBMs) and tenders at Kossel Road, in the Palau Islands, in preparation for the retaking of the Philippines.

Somewhere in the Solomons, a VP-44 Catalina delivers supplies and equipment to a coastwatcher, almost certainly picking up downed fliers in return. Through the first half of 1944, VP-44 operated PBY-5s on 'Black Cat' and Dumbo missions from bases in the Green Islands (*Dave's Warbirds*)

The Palaus had been invaded by the Marine Corps in early September, and FAW 1, having now transferred to USS *Chandeleur*, began extended scouting, reconnaissance and ASR operations into the Philippines from Kossel Road. The tenders involved included USS *Pocomoke*, USS *Yakutat*, USS *Onslow* and USS *Mackinac*. The PBYs of VP-54 were in the vanguard of this operation, and they were joined by the first PBMs to move to the Western Pacific, assigned to VP-216. On 1 November, after a bitter battle for the island, a VPB-54 PBY-5A became the first Allied aircraft to land at Peleliu, establishing a small det there for local Dumbo operations.

FAW 1's VPB-23, operating 15 PBY-5As from Eniwetok, in the Marshalls, transferred a 12-aeroplane detachment to the operational command of CTU 94.4.2/Commander Shore-based Aircraft Marianas aboard *Hamlin*, in Saipan's Tanapag harbour, on 4 December. Three of the Catalinas were immediately sent to Orote Field, on Guam, for Dumbo ASR duties, while two others worked directly with the USAAF performing the same task from Tinian. The remaining seven stayed at Tanapag, although three days later two were detached to Falalo Island, in the Ulithi Atoll chain, for more ASR work. On 27 December two more PBYs were sent to Peleliu to relieve VPB-54 in the Dumbo role.

By 1944, operational commanders had sufficient resources to move aircraft to where they could make the greatest contribution.

RETAKING THE PHILIPPINES

With American forces now firmly established in the Marianas, the Allies were poised to control the seaways south from Japan. Such control meant that the Philippines could now be retaken, and the campaign to achieve this was the goal that brought the Southwest Pacific and the Central Pacific offensives together. With the push for the Philippines, the Dutch East Indies was left increasingly to Australian forces, where RAAF Catalinas also served with great distinction.

US Army assault forces went ashore on Leyte on 17 October, this invasion precipitating the Battle for Leyte Gulf – the last gasp for the IJN.

In a direct link with the dark days of 1941, Rear Admiral Frank Wagner had assumed duties as Commander Aircraft Seventh Fleet on 9 July. This was essentially the same role he had performed as Commander Aircraft Asiatic Fleet in late 1941. The resources available to him in 1944 were, however, many times greater than the two squadrons of PBYs he had had at his disposal almost three years earlier.

USS *Tangier* hoists in a PBY for maintenance while based in Leyte Gulf in late 1944. Usually operating hundreds of miles from adequate support facilities, large tenders such as this vessel were the key to extended seaplane operations in the Pacific War (*US Navy*)

Included in Wagner's force was his former PatWing 10, now designated FAW 10, which moved forward, along with FAW 17, to Woendi, in Dutch New Guinea. Later that month he moved the latter wing, along with VP-11, VP-33 and VP-101, forward from Samarai, to Seeadler harbour. FAW 17 was transferred to Morotai, in the Dutch East Indies, on 19 October, and then to Leyte Gulf, along with the tender *Tangier*, on 30 December. FAW 10, meanwhile, moved to Seeadler aboard USS *Currituck* on 1 September then directly to Leyte Gulf on the heels of the invasion on 17 October in support of the PBY-5s of VP-33 and VP-34. *San Pablo, Half Moon, San Carlos* and *Orca* followed close behind. Wagner, FAW 10 and the US Navy were now back in the Philippines.

VP-34's finest hour came on 3 December in the wake of the torpedoing of the destroyer USS *Cooper* in Ormoc Bay, off Leyte, when many survivors were rescued by its PBYs during the course of several daring flights into hostile waters.

By then the unit was, technically, VPB-34, as on 1 November all VP squadrons had been redesignated patrol bombing units. This was a simple letter change for most outfits, although VP-101 became VPB-29.

PBY production was continuing in New Orleans, but the patrol baton had been passed to other aircraft types. The number of VP/VPB squadrons – by now operating several types of aircraft – reached its peak in October 1944, and thereafter declined as the war drew to a close. A mere two years before, in October 1942, the US Navy had only 20 VP squadrons in commission, all bar two flying PBYs (one had PB2Ys and VP-82 landplanes). At its peak, the US Navy had 77 VP/VPB squadrons, with 38 of them equipped with flying-boats. In the Pacific, there were at least 30 flying-boat squadrons, and 17 of those flew PBY-5/5As.

By the end of 1944, eight PBY-equipped squadrons had been withdrawn from frontline service. For some, of course, it was simply the end of a long combat tour, but for others it meant reassignment. Included in the ranks of the latter were VPBs -11, -12, -14, -29, -34, -52, -72 and -91, all of whom would never fly the PBY again.

It can be said of the Catalina that she was graceful in conceding centre stage to others, and contented herself with the many utility roles that contributed to the welfare and morale of the fighting men and women in forward areas. Besides, lifting in mail from home to isolated and remote commands made the aircraft a star in the minds of the average GIs in the Pacific.

Commissioned into the US Navy in March 1943, the small seaplane tender USS *San Pablo* subsequently saw considerable action in the South Pacific. The vessel spent the final months of the war in the Samar and the Lingayen Gulf areas supporting ASR operations in the South China Sea

'BLACK CATS'

Combat always breeds improvisation amongst those locked in deadly conflict, since no pre-war plan ever survives the opening shot. This was very much the case for the VP crews fighting for their lives in the Dutch East Indies following the invasion of the Philippines in December 1941. Two months after fleeing Manila, PatWing 10 commenced operations at night as a simple expedient to avoid the numerous enemy fighters then roaming the skies.

At much the same time, PatWing 4's squadrons were having their PBYs fitted with British ASV radar in Alameda in the hope that these aircraft could then navigate better in the abominable weather in the Aleutians. Another critical piece of equipment for the PBYs that made its service debut at around this time was the newly-developed radio altimeter, which, rather than depending on air pressure to determine altitude, bounced a radio signal off the ocean's surface to calculate the distance precisely, quickly and continuously. Suddenly, Catalina crews had what they needed to operate the aircraft with confidence at low altitude at night.

PatWing 10's brutal experience at the hands of enemy fighters had revealed just how vulnerable the PBY was. Armour plate panels behind the pilots' seats and in the waist gunners' positions, as well as self-sealing fuel tank liners, helped a little, but the flying-boat remained vulnerable nonetheless. However, the aircraft's great range, ability to perform a variety of useful work both on land and water, fitment with newly-developed radar equipment and significant, and varied, ordnance payload meant that the Catalina still had a lot of operational life left in it.

VP-11, in the Solomons, had begun to experiment with night operations in the autumn of 1942, going as far as to paint its aeroplanes' undersurfaces black to mask their movement in the darkness. Even in these early stages, the 'Black Cat' concept showed promise.

In November, VP-12 had deployed from Hawaii with 12 new, fully equipped, PBY-5As for operations in the South Pacific with FAW 1. The unit was initially sent to Nandi, in the Fiji Islands, and it was from here on 15 December that its commanding officer, Cdr Clarence Taff, flew his newly-repainted, all-black PBY-5A over to Henderson Field – the nickname 'Black Cat' was bestowed on the aircraft shortly after its arrival on Guadalcanal. Within a week, four more flat black-painted flying-boats from Taff's squadron had joined him. From then until the sixth PBY arrived in March, Cdr Taff and his 'Black Cats' completed 236 individual sorties, almost all at night. Typically, his aircraft were armed with up to four 500-lb bombs, and his crews were trained to scout out and report anything and everything they found.

These nocturnal missions brought immediate results, both in terms of information about enemy movements and putting bombs on targets. Inspired by VP-12's efforts, other squadrons began performing night intruder missions too. In the Solomons, conditions for such sorties were literally made to order, and to varying degrees suitably equipped

Pilots Lts Hine (left) and Higgs of VP-11 converse on their well-weathered 'Black Cat' *PISTOL PACKIN' MAMA* at Samarai, in New Guinea, in late 1943. This unit decorated its aircraft with nose art and mission markers – this particular PBY boasted a mission tally of 16 bomb and two torpedo symbols when this photograph was taken (*Dave's Warbirds*)

VP-12's innovative commanding officer, Cdr Clarence O Taff, was the originator of the 'Black Cat' concept. He is seen here relaxing for the camera with 'Yardbird', the squadron's first 'black cat', on Guadalcanal in early 1943 (*Dave's Warbirds*)

Catalinas from VP-11, VP-51 and VP-91 also participated in 'Black Cat' operations.

Single PBYs would launch in the late afternoon, fly all night and then recover the next morning in daylight. Radar for navigation among the many islands was important, although on a clear moonlit night crews usually managed to find their way around without it. For detecting and pinpointing targets, radar was invaluable, although it was the radio altimeter that made such missions possible in the first place. From the air, the sea at night appeared to be little more than a black void, and depth perception for aircrew was a matter of dangerous guesswork. The altimeter became so crucial to 'Black Cat' operations that if it failed, the PBY immediately returned home.

At Henderson Field, adapting available tools to meet requirements often meant survival itself, and so the emergence of the 'Black Cats' here came as no surprise. In daylight, Allied fighter squadrons were gradually achieving air superiority, and so the Japanese, to avoid being attacked from the air, began moving men, supplies and equipment under cover of darkness. This in turn meant that the PBYs were now presented with a target-rich environment during their nightly patrols.

The slow Catalina was well suited to such missions thanks to the wide variety of ordnance – mostly 500-lb demolition bombs, but sometimes torpedoes – that it could carry. Learning quickly to navigate by radar in the darkness, the prowling VP crews hunted the enemy at sea, along the coast, in swamps and on small islands. Every object sighted in moonlight or showing up on radar – the metal structure of a barge or a destroyer made for a solid radar return – was fair game.

Quick to pick up on the 'Black Cat' potential, VP-101 in Western Australia began to be more aggressive during its long patrols over the Dutch East Indies. And as this unit discovered, all a squadron needed to get into the 'Black Cat' business was a PBY, radar, a radio altimeter, some black paint and plenty of ammunition!

In 1943 VP-12 would further refine the night intruder mission by equipping its aircraft with bombs that had been fitted with delayed-action fuses. These in turn allowed PBYs to attack enemy ships at masthead height without blowing themselves out of the sky as a result of the explosion of their own bombs when they struck the target.

As deadly as the Japanese were in the Solomons, as in the Aleutians, the weather was often a more formidable opponent in the Pacific. Tropical storms, squalls and huge thunderheads lead any judicious pilot to immediately alter course in avoidance. Getting around such storms at night presented a serious problem to PBY crews, as their appearance on the radar screen was inconsistent and unreliable.

Flak from enemy shipping also posed a constant threat to 'Black Cats', being both plentiful and fierce, but usually rather ineffective,

Four anonymous 'Black Cats' (including the one in which the photographer is sat) fly in loose formation somewhere in the South Pacific in 1943-44. Seeing 'Black Cat' PBYs in this number during daylight hours usually meant that the squadron involved was moving bases (*US Navy*)

since the gunners needed a visual sighting of the target at which to aim at, and this seldom occurred. The PBYs, of course, never used tracer ammunition in their guns so as to avoid giving away their position. The Japanese caught on quickly and removed all tracer ammunition from their guns too, as although it helped the gunners train onto their targets, it also made them sitting ducks for the prowling 'Black Cats'.

Back in Hawaii, CINCPAC Admiral Nimitz was buoyed by the early reports of VP-12's successes in the Solomons, and quickly saw the potential for hurting the enemy on a wider scale. Responding to his instructions, FAW 2 ordered newly-established VP-54 to prepare for a 'Black Cat' deployment in February 1943. Flying brand new PBY-5As identically configured to those in service with VP-12, the unit's lead elements began departing in early March for service with FAW 1 on Guadalcanal.

The transit was not without its dangers, however, and while at Canton Island, four PBYs were caught on the ground and destroyed in a surprise raid by IJN G4M 'Betty' bombers flying from a base in the occupied Gilbert Islands. Undeterred, VP-54 pressed on and flew its first offensive patrols on 11 March. The unit's crews would absorb all that VP-12 could teach them, and then continue to evolve techniques of their own. Finally, on 1 June VP-54 formally relieved VP-12, allowing the latter unit to return home for refitting.

Nightflying a PBY over enemy territory proved to be a graduate-level challenge for the pilots involved, demanding not a little savvy and presence of mind. The following account on VP-54's operations from Guadalcanal in 1943 came from the unit's war diary;

'During the course of over nine months' operations in the Solomon Islands area by this squadron, various lessons have been learned mostly in connection with night operations. The greatest hazard in nightflying has been found to be the weather. Local squalls can be easily avoided if there is enough starlight or moonlight to detect them, but often bad fronts which are too extensive to go around cover the area. The pilot then has to determine whether to plough through the front or return to base. Eventually, one learns to judge pretty well what he can get through safely and what is impenetrable.

Brand new VP-12 PBY-5A BuNo 48253 is seen with its groundcrew at Henderson Field in January 1944. This aircraft met an untimely ending on 8 March 1944 when it flew into a mountain on Choiseul Island, in the Solomons, during a 'Black Cat' mission. All nine aircrew aboard the PBY perished (*Mel Crocker*)

Looking as good as new, a recently refurbished 'Black Cat' takes off from the RAAF repair base at Lake Boga following the completion of a rework and overhaul. It would not remain in this condition for long once back in the frontline (*Dave's Warbirds*)

'There is one set rule that all our pilots agree on – "Never attempt to climb over any bad weather in a PBY-5A". The aeroplane, with the heavy patrol loading, is very rarely able to gain sufficient altitude to climb over the front, and flying blind at night while climbing through a turbulent frontal area is one almost certain method of becoming confused and hopelessly lost. Experience has proven that it is much safer to attempt to go under the storm at an altitude of 500-1000 ft.

'Virtually all the night navigation in the Solomons was accomplished by use of radar. There are numerous islands and landmarks, so that frequent bearing and distances obtained by use of the radar give accurate fixes. One learns by experience to recognise islands and various landmarks at night by their distinctive contours and silhouettes. However, if one is negligent in his navigation and fails to take frequent checks on his position at 10-15 minute intervals, it is very easy to become confused after making several radical changes in course while avoiding the numerous and frequent squalls.

'Thoroughness in navigation can not be stressed too highly, for you must know your own exact position before you can properly report any enemy contacts. It is also imperative that you at all times know your own exact position in respect to your friendly task forces in the immediate vicinity.'

TARGETS ABOUND

Throughout 1943, there was no shortage of targets for the 'Black Cats', and for good reason. With the loss of Tulagi and Guadalcanal, the Japanese were now seeking to consolidate and defend other positions in the Solomons, moving troops and supplies to various locations, and soon also trying to evacuate personnel from isolated or bypassed islands to fight elsewhere. All these movements had to be made after dark so as to avoid the now ever present Allied dive-bombers that roamed overhead from dawn until dusk. This situation made the Solomon Islands a hunter's paradise for the prowling 'Black Cats'.

This extract from VP-54's war diary reveals how the unit modified its tactics so as to get the best results whilst opposing renewed Japanese offensives;

'At the squadron's suggestion, the "mike search" (following a pre-planned track) was discontinued. A number of more useful night patrols were substituted which took the "Black Cats" deep into enemy territory to hunt for Jap shipping at the top of "the Slot" and off the southwest and northeast coasts of Bougainville.

'At the inception and during the 32-day Rendova and Munda campaigns, the Japs attempted to land reinforcements, to shell our land positions and to oppose Allied task forces. Four to six "Black Cats" were sent out nightly to search for, report and attack Jap warships. Contacts were numerous, and the "Black Cats" were frequently able to guide Allied warships to the Jap forces and to illuminate after the enemy had been engaged.

'The squadron takes pardonable pride in the fact that virtually every major contact with Jap surface forces was first developed by search aeroplanes from VP-54.

'"Black Cat" contacts led to each of the several battles of Kula and Vella Gulfs. In nearly every instance the "Black Cats" dropped their four 500-lb bombs on the ships contacted, or in the event of no contact, bombs were dropped on Vila airfield (a fighter strip on Japanese-held Kolombangara).'

VP-52 'Black Cats' head out at the start of yet another night's work, somewhere over New Guinea in December 1943. The trio of aircraft would soon go their separate ways once the sun had set. VP-52 moved from Perth to Namoia Bay, via Palm Island, in October-November 1943. Using the tender *Heron* for support, the unit flew operations from the Port Moresby area up to the Bismarck Islands until February 1944. VP-52 was subsequently awarded a Presidential Unit Citation for its record in combat during this period (*Dave's Warbirds*)

'Black Cats' typically launched in the evening's failing light and landed shortly after dawn the next morning, with these crucial missions being flown in every conceivable weather condition. The crews almost always successfully completed the missions assigned to them, pressing home bombing and strafing runs despite the inadequacies of their aeroplanes when it came to such operations.

The 'Black Cat' PBYs sent to the Solomon Islands were amongst the best available, but they soon had a high number of flying hours under their belts and began to feel the effects of nightly combat operations. A great deal of credit for their continued operation had to go to the officers and men of PATSU-1 for their work in keeping the 'Black Cats' flying. This unit operated without adequate facilities, equipment or supplies, yet very few flights were turned down by VP-54 for lack of aircraft.

Flying can be an enjoyable experience, but seldom in war, and almost never over the Solomons in 1943. The traffic 'congestion' in the skies over Guadalcanal and 'the Slot' was severe, and the prudent flyer assumed that every contact was enemy until positively identified as friendly. Flying at night in a 'Black Cat' greatly increased the strain and the danger experienced by the crew. Identification of friendly forces was always risky, although Japanese aircraft seldom flew at night. Nevertheless, they had to work out who was who in a gunfire exchange during the frequent naval engagements so common in this theatre, avoid thunderheads, but keep track of nearby mountain peaks, and also quickly work out the best way to identify and then possibly attack the numerous target blips that cropped up on radar – and all this was done at night.

FAW 1 on Guadalcanal orchestrated a 'continuous symphony' in the darkness over the Solomons, with VP-54's nocturnal probing reaching further and further north to the area around Rabaul and even to New Ireland. Rather in desperation, and with their efforts thwarted at every turn, there were a number of attempts by the Japanese to counter the 'Black Cats'. Picket boats were placed in the St George channel, between New Britain and New Ireland, in an effort to detect the approaching intruders low on the water, but these were easily countered when the PBYs simply took alternate routes to their patrol areas.

Decoy ships also appeared, these vessels being armed with a heavy flak battery and showing a good radar return, suggesting that they were large

Guadalcanal-based VP-54 fitted several of its PBY-5As with twin, fixed, 20 mm cannon in the nose in 1943-44. The weapon's rate of fire was slower than the 0.50-cal machine gun, but the hitting power of each of its 'slugs' was far greater (*Dave's Warbirds*)

PBY-5 'Black Cat' #24, squadron unknown, is seen here on the water at Samarai, in New Guinea, with replacement cowlings from a non-Black Cat cohort, on 23 November 1943. VP-52 moved up from Palm Island to Namoia Bay and Samarai that month for 'Black Cat' operations

juicy targets inviting attack. Their effectiveness was marginal, however, since the PBY, making a shallow diving attack with engines throttled back, was essentially invisible to the gunners. Before they knew it, their target would be overhead dropping bombs, followed by magnesium flares to light up the area and blind the gunners. It was, to coin a phrase, a 'cat and mouse game', with the 'Black Cats' holding all the trumps.

Strafing was always a useful form of attack, but the Catalina's single flexible 0.30-cal Browning machine gun in the bow was not nearly what the 'Black Cat' sailors thought sufficient for their needs. Under the circumstances, it was only a matter of time before some creative Naval Aviator began adding to the aircraft's arsenal. One such individual was VP-54 pilot Lt William J Lahodney, who had four 0.50-cal weapons rigged up in the bow compartment to fire forward when triggered by the pilot at an angle nine inches below the horizontal. The installation displaced the Norden bombsight, which was useless for low-level night attacks in any case. Lahodney and his crew found the installation quite utilitarian and very workable, not to say deadly, and they were not alone.

Another crew mounted a pair of yet heavier 20 mm cannon firing forward. In both cases the PBY's slow speed was an advantage, giving the crew more time to saturate the target with bullets.

To appreciate fully the effect that these weapons had on small boats, coasters, transports, barges and even well armed, but unarmoured patrol craft and destroyers, it is helpful to understand that the typical 0.50-cal 'slug' easily penetrated 3/8ths-of-an-inch thick steel plate, ripped through and shattered wooden structures with ease and devastated machinery and equipment of any kind whatsoever. The 0.50-cal gun fired at the rate of about 600 rounds per minute. Therefore, a 'Black Cat' in a masthead attack firing a five-second burst sprayed the target with around 200 pointed steel 'slugs'. The 20 mm cannon fired a little slower, but each round was heavier and more deadly.

By late summer, VP-81 was receiving new PBY-5As from the factory in preparation for deployment to the Solomons following combat training in Hawaii. VP-54 handed over the 'Black Cat' mission to the unit in November and returned home. For the enemy, however, there was no break in the pressure.

'Black Cat' operations quickly garnered a lot of interest, with FAW 17, newly-established in Brisbane in September, kicking off its nocturnal campaign in New Guinea. Its units soon proved to be as effective in this role as squadrons in the Solomons, VP-11 at NAS Palm Island and VP-101, then in Brisbane, both being amongst the most experienced squadrons in-theatre. VP-101 moved forward to Samarai, in New Guinea, in October to get closer to

Four 'Black Cats' off on a job. The insignia says late war, and the aeroplane number on the fin is just visible. From April to June, 1944, VP-33, VP-34, VP-52 and VP-81 all worked the 'Black Cat' circuit

its targets, and VP-33 followed suit later that same month. VP-52 then headed north to Namoia Bay, near Samarai, where it was supported by the tender *San Pablo*. These four squadrons adapted, improvised and very soon began to throttle back Japanese supply efforts.

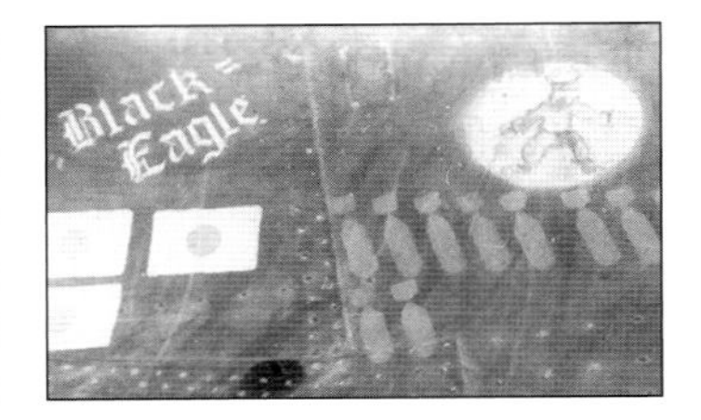

VPB-71 also applied bomb tallies and nicknames to its 'Black Cats' in 1944. *Black Eagle* featured bomb symbols and aerial victory flags, although the latter almost certainly denoted aircraft destroyed on the ground (*Dave's Warbirds*)

VP-33 shuffled over to Perth (FAW 10) to work the Dutch East Indies 'Black Cat' beat, flying from tenders in Exmouth Gulf. Thus relieved, VP-34 shifted from Perth to Palm Island in December so that its aircraft could be overhauled, and after Christmas it headed to Samarai to replace VP-101. Even as the squadrons rotated in and out, FAW 17 maintained the pressure on the enemy, and there were very few nights when numerous 'Black Cats' did not go out on the prowl, endeavouring to be precisely where the enemy did not expect them to be.

Fitted with beaching gear, this VP-44 PBY-5 has been brought up onto the Halavo ramp for refuelling via a bowser pump. The aircraft already has 500-lb bombs loaded under each wing. Harder to make out in the bow is the mounting for four 0.50-cal Brownings in place of the bombsight. Several 'Black Cat' squadrons used both the flying boat and amphibian versions [*Dave's Warbirds*]

By year-end, the 'Black Cats' were spreading havoc on a near-nightly basis from Java, in the west, through New Guinea to New Ireland in the east. Admittedly, their encounters were little more than skirmishes in the grand scheme of things, but as their frequency and numbers increased, their impact became more and more telling. Allied aircraft attacked by day and the 'Black Cats' prowled by night. The PBYs flew irregular tracks at varying times, establishing no distinguishable patterns that would allow the Japanese to effectively target them. There may have been some safe havens, but not many.

1944

One of FAW 1's workhorse units in the Solomons was VP-81 and its PBY-5As on Guadalcanal. The squadron moved a det forward to Munda in February 1944 and began serious work coordinating with PT boat squadrons, before shifting even further forward in March to the new airfield at 'Piva Yoke', which had been carved out of the jungle by SeaBees on Bougainville Island. From this vantage point virtually on Rabaul's doorstep, VP-81 'Black Cats' could cover all the enemy positions in New Britain and New Ireland, with plenty of loiter time available to scour the area for increasingly scarce targets.

In June, VP-81 finally returned to the USA to commence its conversion onto the new PB4Y-2 Privateer as VPB-121.

A 'Black Cat' returns to Samarai following the completion of yet another night's work in 1943-44. Conditions such as these were perfect for PBY operations

Late-model PBY-5A 'B64' of VPB-54 was fitted with a pair of 0.30-cal machine guns in an 'eyeball' bow turret. Note also the radar antenna housed within a protective dome atop the rear cockpit. The radar's performance was greatly improved by locating its antenna in this position, and the housing became a standard fit with the PBY-6A. VPB-54 continued to run 'Black Cat' operations in the Philippines up until February 1945, when the unit was relieved by PBM-equipped VPB-17. The PBY squadron then returned to the US and was disestablished two months later (*Dave's Warbirds*)

Both VP-44 and VP-91 continued to run 'Black Cat' operations from an airfield in the Green Islands, however, until relieved in August.

FAW 10's VP-34 had flown patrols into the Dutch East Indies until replaced on station by the PBY-5s of VP-11 in February, although these long missions had become progressively less productive as targets became more and more scarce and enemy activity decreased. Indeed, VP-11 was soon transferred to FAW 17 at Biak.

The latter wing's 'Black Cats' had been the night-time terror of the New Guinea coast since late 1943, with VP-33 and other units carousing at will. VP-52 jumped forward to operate from USS *Heron* in Humboldt Bay, Hollandia, in the spring of 1944, and by the late summer, FAW 17's VP-101 and VP-11 'Black Cats' had advanced to Morotai. Supported by *San Pablo* and *Orca*, both units sent PBYs probing deep into the Dutch East Indies and the southern Philippines, spreading havoc on a nightly basis. VPB-29 (ex-VP-101) was relieved on 10 November and sent back to the USA, with VPB-11 following four days later.

With Japanese forces reeling from Allied offensives across the Pacific, more and more 'Black Cats' were being transferred home as suitable targets dried up. Finally, in February 1945, the last nocturnal PBY missions in-theatre were flown and the 'Black Cats'' nocturnal prowlings formally came to an end.

Measuring the overall success of the 'Black Cat' force, and the tactics they employed, remains elusive. Some significant portion of the 2.8 million tons of Japanese naval and merchant shipping destroyed by US Navy air attack fell without any doubt to the 'Black Cats', although such figures do not tell the part of the story that is considerably more difficult to assess.

How much sooner, for instance, did enemy commanders concede the untenability of important positions they could no longer support because they could not get supplies through at night? How many lives of invading Allied soldiers were saved because the enemy position, though fiercely defended, was undermanned by troops that were hungry and short on ammunition, medicine and critical supplies? For sure, not all benefits of such an effort are neatly described in statistics and graphs.

A late-model PBY-5 is secured to a red and white striped aircraft mooring buoy somewhere in the Pacific in early 1945. The crew worked the buoy via the hatch forward on the port side, casting off when departing and tying up to the buoy when returning. Such seamanship skills were routinely exhibited by all VP crews, becoming a routine part of their operational readiness when assigned to a PBY squadron. Note the 1945-style national insignia and twin 0.30-cal Brownings in the 'eyeball' bow turret (*Dave's Warbirds*)

DUMBO – AIR SEA RESCUE

From the earliest days of the Pacific War, the Catalina's aquatic abilities made it the premier Allied Air-Sea Rescue (ASR) platform of its day. Indeed, the very first wartime efforts at ASR in-theatre involving PBYs came in the Dutch East Indies in December 1941 and January 1942, involving British, Dutch Navy and PatWing 10 Catalinas. A VP-101 PBY-4 from the latter wing found a squadronmate down in the Celebes Sea south of Jolo during a patrol on 28 December, duly picking up the crew of '101-P-11' (BuNo 1230) as their riddled aeroplane sank. This rescue was made in full sight of Japanese aircraft in the distance.

Several days later, an RAAF Hudson went down in the Molucca Sea, north of Ambon, and an alert radioman in PatWing 10's 'Boat 23' (BuNo 1235) on patrol nearby picked up the call for help and the aircraft's position. Lt John J Hyland and his PBY were on the scene with 30 minutes to rescue sole survivor Sgt B F Hack from the water.

In the aftermath of the Battle of the Coral Sea in May 1942, it was the PBYs from Noumea that located and rescued many survivors from the sunken oiler USS *Neosho* and its escorting destroyer USS *Sims*.

Due to the vastness of the Pacific, the war in this theatre could not help but be one of attrition, and Admiral Nimitz clearly thought in those terms. Operations in the Solomons and New Guinea quickly became precisely that, exacting a heavy toll on men in the frontline. Unlike the enemy, who displayed a foolish, even flagrant, proclivity to squander resources, including the lives of its aviators, soldiers and sailors, the Allies knew that its skilled and effective warriors – especially pilots and aircrew – could not be frittered away if victory was to be achieved. Such personnel required a great investment of time and resources in training and development. Therefore, early on in the conflict, US forces sought means to minimise the loss of pilots and aircrew whenever possible.

From mid-1942, in both the Solomons and New Guinea, the campaign gathered momentum and moved progressively northwards, with the number of aircraft involved increasing many fold as air combat became ever more intense. Inevitably, an increasing number of Allied pilots and aircrew were shot down as the operational tempo grew.

And it was during this ramping up in the Pacific in the autumn of 1942 that ASR missions in the PBY received the 'Dumbo' monicker. Precisely who was responsible for this nickname is not recorded, but the popular Disney film starring the floppy-eared elephant was the inspiration, and once applied by some imaginative sailor, the name stuck.

One of the biggest ASR missions attempted to date occurred in late October 1942 when a USAAF C-47 bound for Henderson from Espiritu Santo ditched on a reef. Three PBYs were soon on the scene – '11-P-9'

A VP-11 PBY crew poses with a recently rescued flyer. This scene was staged back at base for an official US Navy photographer (*Dave's Warbirds*)

(BuNo 2355), '23-P-5' and '51-P-5', and they quickly picked up all the passengers and crew. However, due to the treacherous sea conditions, all three Catalinas were also damaged during the course of the rescue. Unable to take off, the aircraft were abandoned when the destroyer USS *Barton* arrived on the scene. Two of the PBYs were left stranded on the reef and '51-P-5' collided with the ship during the passenger transfer and sank.

Several weeks later, during the Battle of Guadalcanal (12-13 November), the Pacific Fleet took some heavy blows at the hands of the IJN battleships *Hiei* and *Kirishima* near Savo Island. Withdrawing from the area, the crew of the heavy cruiser USS *San Francisco*, its bridge demolished and communications shattered, watched in horror as a torpedo from an enemy submarine approached, missed them and hit the badly damaged light cruiser USS *Juneau*, which sank minutes later. A PBY found six sailors on a raft a few days later, the tender *Ballard* located a seventh and a second PBY retrieved three more off nearby San Christobal Island – only ten survivors from a crew of more than 700. As this rescue proved, the Dumbo was for sailors as well as airmen.

1943

VP-44's Lt Harry Metke and crew took off in '44-P-6' from the tender at Espiritu Santo on the morning of 18 April 1943 and headed for the area west of New Georgia, in the central Solomons, on what to them seemed to be a routine ASR mission. Metke did not particularly care for this assignment, as he knew that Munda, on New Georgia, was home to enemy fighters. Besides, the unit kept a two-PBY det at Halavo for just such local operations, as they were much closer to New Georgia. However, without knowing the overall operational picture on this day – individual crews never did – they simply got on with their assignment.

Ens Johnson was in the right hand seat, the NAP was Frank Michalek, and William Junck, Samuel Minervino, Ed McKissick, Arthur Carson and Charles Marsh filled the remaining positions. The navigator gave Metke a course for their first stop – a small coral lagoon off New Georgia – where they would drop off supplies and equipment for an Australian coast watcher, as well as pick up a downed pilot.

As the PBY neared the appointed landing area, the crew sighted some P-38s. The Catalina was flying at an altitude of less than 500 ft, and the Lightnings were half as low again in an attempt to avoid radar detection by the Japanese. The USAAF fighters were fast, and quickly disappeared in the mists. They too were headed for the northern Solomons. It was a cloudy, overcast day, and the seas were running at six to eight feet.

The PBY landed, made the pick up and delivery and was soon back in the air headed for home when, suddenly, the pilot's radio receiver, tuned as usual to the fighter circuit, erupted with the chatter of a battle. Pilots were calling and yelling to each other, selecting targets. They were successful in downing two bombers, as well as some of the fighter escorts, and the fight ended when the flight leader told his unit to turn for home.

The PBY crew had heard such chatter before, and at this point, with their own mission accomplished, they continued south for home.

Charles Marsh was on watch in the waist hatch, and he had a good view of the events that followed. A damaged P-38 appeared to starboard and made a wide, sweeping turn about half-a-mile away. At the end of the turn, the fighter, which was badly damaged, pulled abeam of the PBY and the two aircraft flew side-by-side at a height of about 700 ft. Marsh reported to his pilot that the Lightning's port engine was stopped and the propeller feathered. There were oil streaks behind the damaged engine, its cowling had been holed by enemy fire and bullets had also hit the fuselage ahead of the cockpit, although the canopy itself seemed to be intact.

Metke was in contact with the pilot by radio, and he asked him if he was all right. After a pause, he answered that he thought so. Metke then questioned him about the serviceability of the fighter's starboard engine, and if he had enough fuel to get home. The pilot said he thought he could make it back. Metke assured him that if he wanted to ditch, the PBY could land and pick him up very easily. After some hesitation, the pilot said he thought that he could make it, and asked for the course to Guadalcanal. Metke put the PBY on course and gave the pilot the correct compass heading. Soon, the wobbly P-38 pulled ahead and out of sight. Metke again set course for Espiritu Santo, and the PBY crew landed late that afternoon, logging 9.9 hours on their mission.

Two days later, the crew was enjoying time out of the aircraft aboard *Curtiss* between sorties when a news announcement was made over the ship's loudspeaker to the effect that high ranking Admiral Isoruku Yamamoto and his staff, flying in two 'Betty' bombers, with a Zero-sen escort, had been shot down. The same morning Metke and his crew had flown to New Georgia, 16 USAAF P-38s had sortied from Guadalcanal on a mission based on signal intelligence intercepts. The Lightning pilots subsequently downed the bomber in which the Commander-in-Chief of the IJN's Combined Fleet was a passenger, taking him to his death.

Was Harry Metke's PBY the Dumbo back up for that mission, and was their flight coordinated somehow in support? They were never told.

IMPROVING THE MISSION

Although ASR work raised morale, not every mission was a success. For example, shortly after the Yamamoto episode, a VP-72 PBY responded to a call and successfully recovered a ditched USAAF fighter pilot. However, upon returning to the seaplane base at Halavo Bay, the Catalina crashed, killing five of its crew. Such tragedies drove all PatWing personnel to improve procedures, coordinate better and develop more advanced facilities to support the PBYs. All hands responded to the need, with American, Australian and New Zealand personnel rallying to the cause.

As an example of this, at Halavo Bay, Commander FAW 1 instructed VP-24, with its dozen PBY-5s, to pass its regular patrol work onto other squadrons in the wing and focus instead on ASR. This led to the refinement of skills and procedures, better coordination, improved communications and, most importantly, an increase in the number of aircrew saved versus those lost. Morale soared.

The sheer volume of near-continuous air combat at this stage in the war was exhausting, and the Allies learned to accept losses in order to inflict even greater suffering on the enemy. It was an economic/industrial production war that the Japanese could never win. From the very beginning, however, efforts to recover trained aircrew whenever possible after they had been shot down or forced to ditch was a high priority for the Allies. Indeed, fighter and bomber crews were always amazed, and thankful, their brethren in vulnerable PBYs would risk their all to pull them out of a tight spot during a Dumbo mission.

And the fighter 'flyboys' regularly showed their appreciation in return. For example, in late 1943 VF-17 'Jolly Rogers', flying F4U Corsairs from a base ashore in the Solomons, covered a PBY landing in the bay off Tonelei Island, in the Shortlands. The crew had been sent to pick up a USAAF P-39 pilot who had ditched after a strike. The enemy ashore figured that the pilot and then the Catalina made for good target practice, and fired at both with every available weapon. The F4U pilots covering the rescue responded with a vengeance, performing repeated sweeps along the shore that thinned and scattered the gun crews. The PBY made the pick up and returned a very pleased soldier home to fly again.

Not all attempted recoveries went so successfully, however. A few weeks later, VF-17's Lt(jg) John Keith ditched late in the day, and calls for a Dumbo resulted in the PBY arriving overhead the downed Naval Aviator at dusk. Despite an extensive search, they were unable to find the pilot in the darkness. A PT boat sent to look for Keith also failed to locate him. Efforts followed at dawn, but to no avail. The Corsair pilot was never recovered.

From this and other similar tragedies, it was soon determined that the best way to effect an immediate rescue was to have a Dumbo PBY orbiting near the scene of the strike that could respond very quickly to any distress call. This, of course, would expose the Catalina to counteraction by enemy fighters. Allied airmen appreciated the Dumbos, and any Japanese fighter going after a PBY was inviting a particularly fierce reception from its bodyguards. Often on strikes, an entire fighter squadron was assigned to cover the Dumbo, and they seldom lost one.

As an illustration of just how busy VP squadrons were flying ASR missions in 1943, between April and November, VP-54's Dumbo crews pulled 52 men from perilous situations – 35 in July alone.

VP-44 joined VP-24 as the second dedicated ASR unit in-theatre in June, and the squadrons soon standardised the way they went about performing the Dumbo mission. The implementation of these procedures meant that ASR operations quickly improved by being flown more promptly, thus keeping combat fliers' morale sustained.

The following month, VP-24 proved its worth to soldiers ashore during the bloody invasion of New Georgia, three PBY-5s lifting wounded Marines of the 1st Raider Battalion out of Enogai Inlet, on Kula Gulf, on 11 July. Lt R L Wadsworth led in BuNo 08154, Lt(jg) R B Blodgett followed in BuNo 08249 and Lt(jg) A M Caldwell, in BuNo 08155, was the last to land. The Naval Air Combat Intelligence Officer at Halavo provided the following account of the mission;

'Landing was made offshore Rice Anchorage at 1645 hrs. Landing barges were observed in the inlet, but there was no indication of the presence of wounded. Three enlisted Marines finally put out from shore in a native canoe and reported there were no wounded at Rice Anchorage, but that they believed there were some at Enogai Inlet. While circling to warm up the engines for take-off, Lt Wadsworth noticed other Marines waving, and a rubber raft putting out from shore. The aeroplane waited until the arrival of the raft and took aboard Lt(jg) S M Fulham, USNR, of the USS *Strong*. It was reported that there were five more survivors from the *Strong*, but there was no time to get them from their position inland.

'The aeroplanes were again airborne at 1715 hrs. While circling for a landing at Enogai Inlet, small-calibre (7.7 mm and 0.50-cal) automatic anti-aircraft fire was directed at the PBYs from a point on shore midway between Enogai Inlet and Biaroko Harbor. Landing was made offshore, entrance point Enogai Inlet at 1725 hrs. Lt Wadsworth's aeroplane approached entrance point where evacuees were stationed, and Marines and natives wading offshore held the aeroplane off the reef while two rubber boats were launched, with two crew members, in order to transfer the wounded. The other two aeroplanes stood by off shore.

'When Lt Wadsworth's aeroplane was loaded, he moved off shore to allow the other two aeroplanes to approach and take aboard the remaining passengers. While transfer from shore was being effected (at about 1820 hrs), two, possibly three, Japanese float biplanes ("Petes") approached Enogai from the direction of Munda. Machine gun fire was heard as they approached, indicating strafing runs were being made on our advanced positions on Dragon's Peninsula.

'Before the defensive guns on the Dumbos could be manned, the "Petes" made three strafing runs from 800 ft down to about 300 ft altitude and dropped one bomb (possibly a 30 "pounder"), which fell 30 ft off the bow (port) of Lt(jg) Blodgett's aeroplane, slightly injuring Ens Macauley and spraying the PBY with fragments which damaged the radio and air speed indicator so that they no longer functioned, and cut small holes in the wings, hull and port wingtip pontoon.

'Defensive gunnery was hampered since one of the 0.50-cal waist guns had been removed from each aeroplane to permit taking aboard stretcher cases. The PBYs were also undermanned, with four crew members from Blodgett's and Caldwell's aeroplanes manning boats bringing evacuees from shore. Guns were quickly replaced, and after being manned by available personnel, including evacuees, they returned the Japanese fire.

'All aeroplanes were airborne by 1855 hrs for Halavo. Smith, W A, AMM2c of Lt(jg) Blodgett's crew, was left ashore, and Sharp, C F, Pfc, of the 1st Marine Raiders, was kept aboard by mistake. Successful night landings at Halavo were made by the three aeroplanes, BuNos 2020, 2055 and 2105 respectively. Some 71 evacuees were returned to Halavo.'

Although the F1M pilots had, on this occasion, exhibited far less skill than their compatriots in the Dutch East Indies some 15 months earlier, PatWing 10 had more than one disastrous encounter with 'Pete' floatplanes over New Georgia. In this particular case, the PBY's self-sealing fuel tank liners had proven to be a lifesaver! Once at the seaplane base at Halavo, the wounded Marines were well looked after in the newly built field hospital constructed by the SeaBees.

A native canoe comes alongside a PBY during a re-supply mission for an Australian coast watcher in the Solomons in late 1942. Human cargo in the form of rescued aircrew would often take the place of the freight during the return leg of these missions (*Dave's Warbirds*)

VP-24 PBYs repeated this mission on 21 July, when Lt(jg) J L Cain led the first three aircraft off at 0620 hrs from Halavo, with the Catalinas of Lt(jg)s Ammen and Means close behind. They landed off Enogai Inlet, discharged their passengers and cargo and loaded up with wounded – Cain 25, Ammen 37 and Means 36. Arriving back at Halavo before noon, the wounded were in the naval hospitals at either Halavo or Tulagi within a few hours of leaving the frontlines.

Seeing the need for additional evacuation flights, the unit responded with three more PBYs. This time VP-24's CO, Lt Cdr W L Richards, led Lt(jg)s R B Blodgett and A L Lane aloft. The first two lifted out 35 and 21 wounded, respectively, including many stretcher cases. Lt(jg) Lane's experience was rather different to that of his squadronmates, however.

Richards and Blodgett had departed Enogai Inlet by 1645 hrs, recovering at Halavo just at sunset at 1840 hrs. The last PBY into the inlet, Lane's PBY was still on the water loading 15 stretcher cases and 17 ambulatory patients when two A6M 'Zekes' appeared overhead and attacked. Each fighter made three passes, riddling the flying-boat with machine gun and cannon 'slugs'. Lane started the engines to manoeuvre, thus presenting a more difficult target, while a crewman returned fire from one of the 0.50-cal machine guns in the waist.

The gunner manning the bow 0.30-cal, the Plane Captain in the tower and one of the stretcher patients were hit by some shell fragments during the attack, but, remarkably, none were seriously wounded.

Two Marine Corps F4Us then appeared out of nowhere and suddenly the 'Zekes' were gone. Lane soon had his PBY off the water and climbing when the oil pressure in his port engine began to drop due to the damage suffered in the strafing attack. He had little choice but to shut it down and return to Enogai Inlet, as landing at Halavo with a full load of passengers after sunset in a damaged aeroplane would have been needlessly risky.

Once back on the water, a stiff breeze drove the PBY onto a nearby reef before the Higgins boat could get a line over to tow it to safety. With effort and ingenuity, the wounded were landed, the holes in the hull and wingtip float stuffed with rags and the hull bailed out. The incoming tide floated the aircraft free, allowing it to be towed to a nearby pier and secured, with a bailing watch aboard until sunlight. Enemy aeroplanes dropped bombs on the island during the night, but without effect, and first thing the following morning, the bullet holes in the oil cooler were patched up. Forty gallons of fuel were then taken aboard and the PBY departed Enogai Inlet at 1025 hrs and arrived at Halavo at 1215 hrs.

Daring, ingenuity, skill and dedication do have their limits as to effecting reality, however, and this entry in the VP-24 War Diary, among many, appeared only a few days after Lane's escape from Enogai Inlet;

'Search for man reported adrift in a raft at position 09-45 degrees south, 156-16 degrees east was undertaken by an aeroplane from VP-24, flown by Lt Cdr Richards, with take-off time at 1035 hrs on 1 August. The PBY arrived on station without fighter escort at 1215 hrs and searched an area of 75 miles in length and 50 miles wide downwind from the reported position of the raft, making parallel crosswind sweeps. At 1515 hrs the PBY returned to Halavo, reporting negative results.'

More often than not, however, most ASR flights proved to be both successful and rewarding. On 3 August, Lt(jg) Lane, almost certainly in a different PBY from the one used at Enogai Inlet, lifted in 2000 lbs of supplies to an Australian coast watcher at Ringana, on Choiseul Island. The PBY was off early, picked up its escort of eight USAAF P-40s over 'Fighter 2' on Guadalcanal and headed for its destination. Under the Warhawks' protection, Lane landed in the sheltered water between the islands, delivered the supplies and took aboard four passengers. The latter were F4U fighter pilot 1Lt S O Hall of VMF 213, who had been on the island for two weeks after a 'Zeke' had shot him down, and VT-21 TBF crew Ens M Lawty, ARM3c J Stott and AOM3c J Waldheim.

The CO of FAW 1 ordered VP-23, then at Espiritu Santo, to move forward to Halavo to relieve VP-24 of the ASR mission in late August. The latter unit returned to San Diego for a breather and new aircraft.

There was no let up for VP-23 and VP-14, or other Allied squadrons in-theatre, as the following entry in the log of the Naval Air Combat Intelligence Officer (NACIO) at Halavo for 8 January 1944 records;

'At 0830 hrs, Dumbo under Lt R E McAllister, USNR, of VP-14 departed Rendova with a cover of four B-24s and two B-25s to southeast Choiseul to search for the crew of a crashed B-24. Having covered the area thoroughly with negative results, Dumbo, of its own initiative, proceeded to northern Choiseul, and there spotted a smoke flare on Liana Island.

'At about 1000 hrs, the PBY landed in a sheltered area near the southern shores and the entire crew of the B-24 were rescued. Of these 11 men, two were stretcher cases and several had minor injuries. After Dumbo's radioman insured destruction or concealment of life rafts and other gear which might attract subsequent attention, take off was at 1030 hrs and the aeroplane landed at Rendova about 1145 hrs. Here, the rescued were transferred to a seaplane tender and medical attention given.

'Throughout the entire flight, rough weather and unfavourable flying and landing conditions prevailed. Visibility was below three miles, and low overcast was penetrated by squalls. While landing at Rendova with white caps and high running swells, four rivets were snapped, necessitating temporary repairs while the B-24 crew was being removed.'

The same NACIO log recalled another VP-14 mission on 24 January;

'With Lt B Smith in command, VP-14's "Boat 22" took off at 1400 hrs from Treasury for Tokorina. When in the vicinity of the latter base, orders were received to proceed to position 05-50 degrees south, 153-30 degrees east under an escort of nine F4Us and two SBDs to search for the crew of a TBF reported in the water.

'After half-an-hour of searching, three survivors were located in a raft near the designated position, the attention of Dumbo having been attracted by a smoke bomb. The rescue aeroplane landed at 1730 hrs, survivors were taken aboard and the returning hop was made to base, where they were transferred to the seaplane tender at Treasury.

'Rescued were 1Lt Arthur A Johnston, USMCR, Pvt Vernon H Villalobos, USMC, and Pvt Raymond G Czarnecki, USMC, all attached to a Marine Corps torpedo squadron at Munda. Their aeroplane had been hit by anti-aircraft fire over Rabaul and they had been forced down 20-25 miles south of Cape St George on the 23 January strike. They had hoisted a sail on the raft to prevent the current from carrying them northward to enemy territory, and had travelled 45 miles south-southeast by the time of their rescue.'

VP-74's PBY-5 'Boat 4' undergoes routine maintenance at Halavo in 1944. This particular seaplane base was built by the Seabees from scratch, and was the focal point for much repair and maintenance work in the Solomons

The NACIO log includes similar, multiple Dumbo entries for most days during this period. A report to Commander, Air Forces Solomons described the 17 March rescue flight by Lt Cdr F R Drake, as he and his VP-12 PBY crew found John E Carey of VC-40 off Bougainville;

'Proceeding east of the Treasury Islands, Drake heard SBDs reporting an aeroplane down and calling for a Dumbo and crash boat. Investigating, he saw a man in a life raft waving his arms. Coming about he landed into the wind, but could not see the raft. Taxiing in search, Drake found a man in a life jacket, whom he picked up. Unable to see the originally sighted raft, and observing the bad physical condition of the rescued man, he took off. During this event there was an SBD circling.

'After taking off and heading for Sterling (the main island in the Treasury group southwest of Bougainville, and site of a new Allied airstrip), Drake passed over the crash boat *Mack*, which had been directed to the scene by Carrier Base. The *Mack* called "10B84" (the PBY's voice radio call sign) and asked if they could render assistance. Drake replied that there was another man in the water where the SBD was circling. Distance of *Mack* to the spot was about five miles. Observing another PBY-5 approaching from the direction of Sterling, Mack continued to the base, where he discharged the rescued man.'

The Dumbo crews continued to fly missions like this throughout 1944 and into early 1945, operating closely with Allied fighter and bomber squadrons. Perfecting ASR techniques as the war progressed, the dedicated US Navy Dumbo units continued to include PBYs in their ranks, although as new VH (ASR) squadrons arrived in-theatre from late 1944 onwards, PBMs began augmenting the Catalinas. The latter, however, were never fully replaced.

A PBY Dumbo comes in on finals – the most beautiful sight in the world for a downed aviator in the water being shot at by enemy troops from a nearby beach (*Dave's Warbirds*)

USAAF emergency rescue squadrons, based on the US Navy's experience with the flying-boat units dedicated to ASR, also reached the Pacific from late 1944 onwards, using PBY-5As designated as OA-10As. These aircraft were often augmented by other land-based types such as the B-17 and B-29, the latter dubbed the 'Superdumbo'.

VICTORY IN THE PACIFIC

By January 1945, victory clearly lay ahead for the Allies in the Pacific. There was still much fighting to be done, however, and the PBY remained in action through to VJ-Day, although in ever decreasing numbers.

This PBY-5A was seen in transit at US Coast Guard Air Station San Francisco on its way out to join the Pacific Fleet in late 1945. Note the long range ferry tanks fitted under the aircraft's wings (*Naval Institute*)

The last months of the war saw the Pacific Fleet heavily involved in supporting the island-hopping campaign that had brought the Allies to within sight of the Japanese home islands. PBYs patrolled, rescued and patrolled some more, as airpower wore down the once mighty IJN. There was nothing VPB crews could do to stop *kamikaze* attacks on Allied naval ships, but routine patrols supporting aircraft protecting the fleet, or flying long distances to attack targets in enemy territory, remained important.

By February the Philippines were finally secured, and Okinawa and Iwo Jima came under US control. That same month, VPB-23 (equipped with 15 PBY-5As) sent a detachment of aircraft to the latter island, adding to the dets it was already running at Kobler Field, on Saipan, Falalo Island, Ulithi and Peleliu. ASR continued to be big business for the flying-boat squadrons, and the PBYs were very effective in this role.

As illustrated by VPB-23, in the final months of the war VPB units seldom operated in their entirety from one base. Instead, they were typically split up into several detachments of a few PBYs each, with these dets performing designated tasks for just a brief period of time before being transferred to another location. Tactically, this meant that the units were incredibly flexible when it came to conducting VPB operations.

VPB-53 was yet another PBY unit that split its aircraft up during the summer of 1945, running detachments on Samar Island, in the Philippines, and on Tinian and Guam, in the Marianas. At the same time additional squadron personnel and aeroplanes were heading west into the frontline from Hawaii. One section, which included Lt George R Crumpler and his crew in their brand new PBY-6A BuNo 64037, flew from Kaneohe to Johnson, thence to Guadalcanal, then the Green Islands, and via Seeadler to Biak, in New Guinea, and finally forward to Samar, to join the VPB-53 detachment there for Dumbo operations.

A factory-fresh PBY-6A from Consolidated's New Orleans plant rests between flights at a naval air station somewhere on the west coast of the USA. All PBY-6As came with 'eyeball' bow twin 0.30-cal turrets and the radar housed in a radome just aft of the cockpit (*Naval Institute*)

Assigned to a utility squadron on Guam, this PBY-6A was photographed looking very much like a 'Black Cat' in 1946 (*US Navy*)

Effective 1 July, VPB-53, with a mixed complement of PBY-5/5As, transferred to newly established FAW 18 on Guam, and between the 25th and 27th of that month, the unit received 11 more new PBY-6As ferried in from Hawaii. It added these to its five best PBY-5As and sent the remaining Catalinas home.

On 2 August, in response to the sinking of the heavy cruiser USS *Indianapolis* by the submarine I-53, VPB-53 hastily transferred to Commander, Philippine Sea Frontier, and started flying ASR missions round the clock. Lt Watson and Lt(jg)s Kennedy and McDonald flew that very night to the last known position of the vessel in the Philippines Sea to attempt to locate survivors by illuminating the surface with flares. Once these had been found, crews dropped rafts, food, water and radios. For three days, concluding on the 4th, VPB-53 and several other units flew round the clock to search out and rescue survivors in the open ocean.

PRODUCTION CUT

The US Navy cancelled much of its contracted PBY-6A production at Consolidated's new plant in New Orleans, and the 184th PBY to leave the assembly line in September 1945 was the last Catalina built. As the war came to an end, the number of units using PBYs drew down too.

US Navy unit listings for the Pacific Theatre show just eight squadrons flying Catalinas on VJ-Day. FAW 10 on Palawan had three, VPB-53 was flying 20 PBY-5As from both Manus and Samar, and was receiving new PBY-6As, and both VPB-62 and VPB-71 had yet more PBY-5As also on Samar. In the Aleutians, FAW 4 on Attu had VPB-43 on Adak being relieved by VPB-61 with PBY-5As and four Boeing-built PB2B-1 Catalinas. VPB-43 returned to Seattle to disestablish on 15 September. FAW 18 on Tinian had both VPB-23's 14 PBY-5As scattered between Ulithi, Guam, Peleliu and Saipan, and ASR unit VH-2 with six PB2B-2s on Saipan. In Hawaii, FAW 2's replacement training squadron VPB-100, had a mixed fleet of 24 PBY-5s, -5As and -6As, but clearly its aircrew emphasis was on the 66 PBMs assigned to the unit.

Even in the utility role the Catalina was passing quickly from the scene, as there were now faster and more modern aircraft available. Several commands retained a PBY-5A on staff, including CFAW 1 at Kerama Retto, on Okinawa, COMAIRSEVENTHFLT at Samar and Commander Air Force South Pacific at Noumea. CFAW 8 at Alameda had no fewer than eight PBY-5As and -6As, CFAW 6 at Whidbey Island six PBY-5As, CFAW 10 on Palawan three and CFAW 4 on Attu four. Various utility (VJ-1, -9, -12, -13 and -14), service and training units employed another 24, all bar two of them PBY-5As. In several cases, PBYs operated by these squadrons found PoW camps immediately post-war and airdropped food and clothing for the occupants ahead of their liberation.

Near-new PBY-6As served on with the US Navy's Pacific Fleet utility units until 1948, by which time there were just five in frontline service. A few more enjoyed fruitful employment with the US Navy Reserve, and the US Coast Guard remained a Catalina operator well into the 1950s.

Recently released PoWs – US, British and Dutch – celebrate their freedom at Aomori, in Japan, in September 1945. PBYs, as well as other transports and bombers, searched for PoW camps and dropped supplies to their starving inmates immediately after VJ-Day

COLOUR PLATES

1
PBY-2 BuNo 0490 of VP-10, NAS Pearl Harbor, July 1939
VP-10 was a PatWing 2 unit between 1937-39, and its aircraft featured rudders painted in a solid colour. The rudder marking on this PBY denotes that it had been transferred in to PatWing 2 from PatWing 4 in early 1939. VP-10 became VP-25 and then VP-23, and eventually replaced its PBY-2s with PBY-5s in San Diego in November 1941. BuNo 0490 was posted to a Florida-based training unit in 1942, and was written off in a landing accident in Peridido Bay on 21 June 1944.

2
PBY-3 BuNo 0858 of VP-22, Darwin, Northern Territory, August 1941
This aircraft was one of two VP-22 PBY-3s that carried out the clandestine South Pacific survey flights in August 1941. These aircraft flew from NAS Pearl Harbor to Darwin via various locations in the South Pacific. BuNo 0858 was Lt Tom Moorer's plane, with AMM3c Chuck Baggarly as its Plane Captain. The latter recalled that the flight was a 'real adventure' for all involved. '22-P-10' was later destroyed on the ramp at NAS Ford Island on the morning of 7 December 1941.

3
PBY-3 BuNo unknown of VP-21, Midway Island, December 1941
VP-21 was one of the last PBY-3 units in the Pacific Fleet by late 1941, and it forward deployed from NAS Pearl Harbor to Midway Island so as to fly early warning patrols over the Pacific Ocean in search of IJN warships. In an effort to avoid detection by the unit, the Pearl Harbor Strike Force had to sail even further north. PBYs from VP-21 and VP-22 covered huge expanses of the Pacific in the weeks prior to the Pearl Harbor attack, but still the Japanese force evaded detection.

4
PBY-4 BuNo 1235 of VP-1, NAS North Island, March 1939
The 15th of 19 PBY-4s assigned to VP-1, this flying-boat was delivered to the unit on 19 January 1939 directly from the Consolidated factory already marked up as the squadron commander's aircraft. VP-1 became VP-21 on the eve of its return to Pearl Harbor on 1 July, and BuNo 1235 completed the trip between Hawaii and the Philippines three times following the establishment of the Neutrality Patrol in September 1939. The PBY later served as VP-102's 'Boat 23', performing many useful patrols in the Dutch East Indies during the dark days of 1941-42. Unable to get its engines serviced, BuNo 1235 eventually suffered a mechanical failure in flight in January 1942 and ended up in the surf off a Timor beach with its hull split open.

5
PBY-4 BuNo 1242 of VP-18, NAS North Island, May 1939
Accepted from the factory by PatWing 2's VP-18 in May 1939, this aircraft was one of the first PBYs to feature the new blister enclosures at its waist. The PBY immediately took up the leadership of the squadron's second division as '18-P-7'. PatWing 1 then took control of the unit and redesignated it VP-13, by which time it boasted the wing's double horizontal willow green rudder stripes. The unit was soon returned to PatWing 2 on 1 July 1939, whereupon it was redesignated VP-26 and sent to Pearl Harbor. BuNo 1242 was subsequently transferred to VP-102 in the Philippines in December 1940, becoming '102-P-1'. It was camouflaged the following year, and served as 'Boat 16' until destroyed on the water, along with six other PBYs, in a strafing attack by IJN fighters on Olongapo, Subic Bay, on 12 December 1941.

6
PBY-4 BuNo 1219 of VP-13, NAS North Island, summer 1939
Delivered to VP-18 on 4 November 1938, this aircraft wears VP-13 colours following the squadron's redesignation, although its markings are inconsistent. The green half-cowlings suggest that this PBY was delivered as '18-P-15', and when two other flying-boats left the unit it was renumbered '13-P-13'. The flying-boat was later sent to Hawaii with VP-26 and eventually became VP-101's 'Boat 3', and it was in his guise that it flew Royal Navy Admiral Sir Tom Phillips back to Singapore after his conference with Asiatic Fleet commander Admiral Thomas Hart in the Philippines in early December 1941. The aircraft flew and fought in the Dutch East Indies, before being abandoned with a bad engine at Tjilatjap, in Java, in March 1942. Repaired by a Dutch Navy crew and kept as Y 3, the aircraft eventually made it to Australia, where it was overhauled and impressed into service with the RAAF as A24-28. The Catalina survived the war and was sold to Kingsford Smith Flying Services in 1946.

7
PBY-4 BuNo 1227 of VP-21, Sangley Point, the Philippines, January 1940
This aircraft wears full Neutrality Patrol livery, bar an aviation insignia on the bow (authorised in December 1939), as used by the Asiatic Fleet. Later transferred to VP-102 as 'Boat 26', BuNo 1227 patrolled and fought until Japanese fighters set it afire on the water at Broome on 3 March 1942.

8
PBY-4 BuNo 1216 of VP-21, Sangley Point, the Philippines, early 1940
Marked with its aviation insignia on the bow and

national ensign on the hull decking and under the outer wing panels, this PBY is in typical Asiatic Fleet Neutrality Patrol colours. As the fourth (Black) section leader's aeroplane, it also has a band around the hull aft and full cowl rings. VP-21's aircraft had red rudder colours up until 1 September 1940. The black anti-fouling boot topping synonymous with pre-war PBYs was deleted on Asiatic Fleet Catalinas after the Sangley Point seaplane ramp was finished in January 1940. See plate 13 for the rest of BuNo 1216's history.

9

PBY-4 BuNo 1240 of VP-1, Sangley Point, the Philippines, September 1940

VP-1 chose not to adopt VP-21's red rudder flash when it joined the Asiatic Fleet in December 1940, instead adorning its PBYs with a blue-white-red marking instead, as well as full Neutrality Patrol detailing. '1-P-6' was the third aeroplane in the second (White) section. VP-1 became VP-101 in December 1940 upon the formation of PatWing 10. One year later, BuNo 1240, now in full camouflage, was shot down in flames by Japanese fighters over Jolo Island on 27 December 1941.

10

PBY-4 BuNo 1224 of VP-102, Sangley Point, the Philippines, early 1941

This aircraft was initially assigned to VP-26 at NAS Pearl Harbor, and it was sent to the Philippines along with the rest of the unit in December 1940 to serve with PatWing 10. Once at Sangley Point the squadron was redesignated as VP-102, with VP-1 becoming VP-101. VP-102's PBYs remained 'slick bottomed', lacking the waterline stripe that was a feature of VP-101 aircraft at that time. Note that the PBY also has the Asiatic Fleet rudder flash and Neutrality Patrol markings.

11

PBY-4 BuNo 1238 of VP-101, Sangley Point, the Philippines, 1941

The Asiatic Fleet CINC, Admiral Hart, sensing that war in the Pacific was very near, directed that PatWing 10 devise a camouflage scheme for its PBYs. Work began on repainting all Catalinas in the Philippines in early 1941 – an undocumented process, save for a few photographs and the odd mention in unit operational records. Shades of grey, blue and green were used, with every aeroplane evidently having its own unique pattern and colouring. Extensive Neutrality Patrol work continued throughout this period, although by early 1941 VP units were also flying early warning patrol and scouting missions for the Asiatic Fleet. The bow gunner in this particular PBY, Chief Earl D Payne, gets credit for downing the first Zero-sen to fall to a US Navy aircraft in aerial combat. See the cover artwork caption for further details.

12

PBY-4 BuNo 1226 of VP-101, Naval Station Subic Bay, the Philippines, late 1941

Initially delivered to VP-18 in December 1938, BuNo 1226 subsequently served with VP-13, VP-26 and VP-102 (as '2-P-7'). It was camouflaged while still flying with the latter unit in 1941, receiving the identity 'Boat 22'. The aircraft's crew dropped wreaths over the South China Sea on Memorial Day in 1941 in remembrance of the many servicemen lost at sea. One of the PBYs withdrawn to the Dutch East Indies in December, BuNo 1226 retreated further south until it was finally abandoned in late January 1942 when an over-hours engine failed on patrol and the aircraft could not be repaired in time for it to escape capture by advancing enemy troops.

13

PBY-4 BuNo 1216 of VP-101, Ambon, Java, February 1942

Also the subject of profile 8, BuNo 1216 flew on a number of memorable missions with VP-101 during the early stages of the Pacific War. Having previously served with VP-102, the aircraft participated in the bombing of an IJN battleship, the Jolo Raid and countless patrols from Ambon, on Java. Indeed, it performed PatWing 10's last patrol over the Java Sea on 27-28 February 1942 – the night of the famous battle of the same name. It then evacuated Admiral William Glassford and other senior naval officers to Australia. Renumbered 'Boat 15' in April, the aircraft was sent to the RAAF facility at Rathmines for a well deserved overhaul in June 1942 following several months of frontline flying from Darwin. BuNo 1216 was then transferred to the RAAF as A24-29, and was later one of 11 surplus Catalinas sold to Kingsford Smith Flying Services in 1946.

14

PBY-4 BuNo 1243 of VP-101, Ambon, Java, February 1942

The third of three PBY-4s fitted with blisters in the waist by Consolidated and delivered to VP-18 in May 1939, BuNo 1243 was serving with VP-101 when it carried USAAF General Lewis Brereton and his staff from Luzon to Java on Christmas Day 1941. It then fought throughout the Dutch East Indies campaign, and made several evacuation flights from Java to Australia. It finally succumbed to Japanese fighters when attacked whilst on the water at Broome on 3 March 1942.

15

PBY-4 BuNo 1241 of VP-13, NAS North Island, July 1939

Also modified with blisters, BuNo 1241 remained behind at NAS North Island when VP-13 (ex-VP-18) returned to Hawaii to become VP-26. The aircraft was made available to the contractor for further development work, and it quickly lost its former squadron's logo forward and had the de-icer boots in the wing leading edges painted over. BuNo 1241 was the only one of the three to get a straight trailing edge rudder, and in this form it became the prototype for the PBY-5. Sister PBY-4 BuNo 1245 had no blisters but amphibious landing gear, and was redesignated XPBY-5A.

16
PBY-5 BuNo unknown of VP-12, NAS Kaneohe, December 1941

VP-12 received 12 brand new PBY-5s in the late summer of 1941, all in the BuNo series 2424 through 2444, and then moved west to the new naval air station at Kaneohe, in Hawaii – it was the first PBY squadron to be based here. One of the many casualties of 7 December 1941, bombs, bullets and fire destroyed this aircraft, and numerous others, on the ramp.

17
PBY-5 BuNo 2419 of VP-14, NAS Kaneohe, December 1941

VP-14's crew, with Ens William Tanner commanding, fired the United States' first shot of the Pacific War when they dropped live depth charges on an IJN midget submarine in the defensive area off the entrance to Pearl Harbor more than an hour before Japanese aeroplanes attacked the Pacific Fleet on 7 December 1941.

18
PBY-5 BuNo 2446 of VP-101, Perth, Western Australia, April 1942

VP-23 flew back to Pearl Harbor from San Diego in November 1941 with 12 brand new PBY-5s, and all these of aircraft were either badly damaged or totally destroyed on Ford Island early the following month. BuNo 2446 was rebuilt from pieces salvaged from other PBYs and eventually reissued to VP-21 as '21-P-1'. The aircraft led the squadron to Perth to join PatWing 10 in April 1942, where it was renumbered simply as 'Boat 1' once assigned to VP-101. Lt(jg) Tom Pollock flew the PBY on an extraordinarily daring flight with medicine and ammunition via Darwin to Corregidor just before the island surrendered in late April. Still serving with VP-101 into 1943, the PBY was lost in action over New Guinea in August of that year.

19
PBY-5 BuNo 2292 of VP-101, Darwin, Northern Territory, February 1942

This aircraft was serving with VP-51 at NAS Norfolk, Virginia, when Pearl Harbor was attacked. It was flown to Hawaii as a replacement PBY just days after the raid and issued to VP-22 ('22-P-2'), and the following month the squadron flew across the Pacific to join PatWing 10 in Darwin. Operating from the tender USS *William B Preston*, anchored in Darwin harbour, the aircraft launched (with Lt(jg) Robert C LeFever at the controls) on 19 February for a patrol over Timor. Some 240 miles north-northwest of Darwin, the PBY spotted IJN carriers in heavy weather and reported their location to the tender. Aeroplanes from those carriers were at that very moment bombing Darwin, and *William B Preston* itself. Having survived its various experiences in the frontline, BuNo 2292 cycled back to a Gulf Coast training squadron in 1942 and was eventually scrapped.

20
PBY-5 BuNo 2306 of VP-101, Darwin, Northern Territory, February 1942

Like BuNo 2292, this ex-VP-51 aeroplane was also passed on to VP-22 and survived daring operations in the Dutch East Indies with VP-101. On 19 February 1942, when Lt Thomas H Moorer and crew departed *William B Preston* to scout enemy forces at Ambon, Zero-sens from the IJN carriers *Kaga* and *Hiryu* found the PBY on its outward journey. Their first pass left the Catalina with burning fuel streaming from its ruptured port wing tanks. The pilot, later Chief of Naval Operations and a two term Chairman of the Joint Chiefs of Staff, managed to get his badly shot-up PBY down on the water so the crew could get out safely. In an interview conducted many years later with crewmember AOM2c Ted Lebaron, Admiral Moorer remembered with eyes wide, and leaning to one side in his chair for emphasis, 'It was a very hot fire!'

21
PBY-5 BuNo 2298 of VP-11, on loan to VP-14, Noumea, New Caledonia, February 1942

Most of the few PBYs that survived the devastation at Pearl Harbor gathered under VP-14's wing in the aftermath of the attack. The squadron duly headed south in January 1942 to commence patrols from Suva, on Fiji, and Noumea, in New Caledonia. VP-11 loaned '11-P-7' to VP-14, the aircraft flying patrols from the tenders *Curtiss* and then *Tangier* by February. The markings worn by the aircraft during this period reflect Pacific Fleet reaction to aircraft identification anxieties following the Pearl Harbor attack, red and white rudder stripes and more prominent display of the national insignia being obvious additions. By May 1942 the red ball centre in the insignia had been deleted, and the rudder stripes soon followed.

22
PBY-5 BuNo unknown of VP-43, Dutch Harbor, Alaska, November 1942

For those who fought the war in the Aleutian Islands, the weather was as formidable an opponent as the Japanese. And one of its victims was VP-43's 'Boat 25', which was flipped over on the apron at Dutch Harbor by a 'Williwaw' – a local name among the Aleuts for a 'stiff breeze' that frequents the area – whilst sat on beaching gear.

23
PBY-5A BuNo 48258 of VP-52, Namoia Bay, New Guinea, January 1944

The ever increasing strength of Allied air power made daylight movement of troops and supplies impossible for the Japanese by late 1943, so they tried to transport men and materiel by night. The VP units adapted their tactics too, and 'Black Cats' prowled stealthily throughout the hours of darkness wherever they pleased, from the Solomons to the Celebes Sea. VP-52 was amongst the most successful 'Black Cat' units, being awarded a Presidential Unit Citation for its efforts operating from the Port Moresby area in 1943-44.

24

PBY-5 BuNo unknown of VP-71, Halavo Seaplane Base, Solomon Islands, late 1943

By 1943, individual aeroplane numbering was irregular and often spotty amongst frontline VP units in the Pacific. The gruelling pace of long hours on patrol, or searching for a downed pilot and crew, escorting a convoy, delivering supplies to remote coast watchers, lifting out wounded and other utility work, and little more than a tent in the tropical humidity to call home, left crews little time for recreation. Halavo seaplane base on Florida Island, near Tulagi, was a major repair base through to the end of the war, supporting neutralisation of Rabaul. It also had facilities for crew rest and recreation too. Assigned to FAW 1 in late 1943, VP-71 was operating alongside VP-14 from Halavo at this time.

25

PBY-5A BuNo unknown of VP-81, Munda, Solomon Islands, early 1944

There was very little the Japanese could do about 'Black Cat' attacks from aircraft such as this VP-81 PBY-5A. They arrived over their targets in the dead of night unannounced, dropped their bombs and were then gone again. There was no escaping detection, as the Catalinas were equipped with radar that gave their crew eyes in the night sky. Defending gunners, however, had no such aids when it came to finding their elusive foes. Like most 'Black Cats' in 1944, this aircraft had twin 0.30-cal machine guns in an 'eyeball' bow turret.

26

PBY-5 BuNo unknown of VPB-71, Samar, the Philippines, late 1944

This VPB-71 'Black Cat', christened *Black Eagle*, was one of a handful to feature both nose art and a mission tally. It saw plenty of action during the bitter fighting to retake the Philippines.

27

PBY-5A BuNo unknown of COMAIRSOPAC, Henderson Field, Guadalcanal, August 1942

Commanding all US Navy, Marine Corps and USAAF aircraft in the South Pacific area, Vice Admiral John S McCain was a capable leader at a crucial time in the Pacific War. He used this PBY-5A as his command flagship, and had it fly critical supplies into Henderson Field just five days after the Marines had first gone ashore on Guadalcanal.

28

PBY-5 BuNo unknown of VP-11, Samarai, New Guinea, December 1943

Another PBY-5 'Black Cat' to feature nose art and a mission tally, *PISTOL PACKIN' MAMA* of VP-11 flew from Samarai, in New Guinea, with newly established FAW 17 from 15 September 1943. The 'body count' kept by its crew confirms that the aircraft had participated in 16 bombing and two torpedo attacks, and nobody bothered to note the huge quantity of machine gun ammunition expended. VP-11 was initially supported by the tender *San Pablo*, which was in turn relieved by *Half Moon* in October. VP-101 joined VP-11 at Samarai in December, and the latter unit was pulled out of the frontline in February 1944.

29

PBY-5 BuNo unknown of VP-11, Samarai, New Guinea, early 1944

This more anonymous VP-11 PBY-5 featured cowlings from a conventionally painted PBY when it received replacement Pratt & Whitney R-1830-92s during an overhaul. The Twin Wasp was a fine engine, but after some 300 to 400 flying hours they would need a thorough overhaul. Maintenance crews in-theatre, functioning with a minimum of gear, did this job well, and often.

30

PBY-5 BuNo unknown of VP-52, Samarai, New Guinea, early 1944

Another anonymous 'Black Cat', this aircraft also flew from Samarai in the early months of 1944. From late 1942, the PBY's nocturnal offensive really began to gather pace, with more and more squadrons being tasked with this mission. Units known to have flown 'Black Cat' missions in the Pacific theatre were VP/VPBs -11, -12, -24, -33, -34, -44, -52, -54, -71, -81, -91 and -101/29 .

31

PBY-5A BuNo unknown of VP-52, Hollandia, New Guinea, spring 1944

The PBY-5A amphibian added a great deal of flexibility to 'Black Cat' operations, and a small number of the amphibians were flown by VP-52 alongside its PBY-5s. With late war insignia and the minimum of markings, this aircraft was typical of the many used by several New Guinea-based squadrons at the time. VP-52 commenced operations from the tender *Half Moon* near Samarai in late January 1944, before moving forward to Humboldt Bay, off Hollandia, and thence to Seeadler with *Tangier*.

32

PBY-6A BuNo unknown of VJ-9, NAS Agaña, Guam, early 1946

Some New Orleans-built PBY-6As made it out to units in the Pacific before VJ-Day, but not this aircraft, marked up as a 'Black Cat'. Assigned to Utility Squadron (VJ) 9 at NAS Agaña, on Guam, the PBY had an 'eyeball' bow turret, fitted with twin 0.30-cal machine guns, and the radar dome above the flightdeck. A number of very similar Boeing PB2B-2s were also issued to Air Sea Rescue Squadron (VH) 2.

INDEX

References to illustrations are shown in **bold**. Plates are shown with page and caption locators in brackets.